O
LLE

ticism

A Critical Guide to
HERMAN MELVILLE

Abstracts of Forty Years of Criticism

JAMES K. BOWEN
Southern Oregon College

RICHARD VANDERBEETS
San Jose State College

Scott, Foresman and Company
Glenview, Illinois   London

813.2
B 67 c
7 785·5
Mar. 1972

Starred (*) abstracts are author-prepared and were first published in *American Litera-ture Abstracts,* volumes I and II (copyright ©1967, 1968, 1969 by the editors of *American Literature Abstracts*). Reprinted with the permission of *American Litera-ture Abstracts.* Independently prepared abstracts were contributed by Carol McMillen Benson and Edward Huggins, of the Research Staff of *American Literature Abstracts.*

Preface

More informative than mere annotated bibliography yet more inclusive and practical than collections of full-length articles, *A Critical Guide to Herman Melville* offers abstracts—concise, accurate, and readable summaries—of over one hundred critical essays bearing on the interpretation and analysis of Melville's novels, tales, and poetry. The abstracts collected here approximate the format and length prescribed by *American Literature Abstracts,* are sufficiently extensive to present the essential content of the material abstracted—thesis, method, outline of substantiation—and to serve as detailed and reliable guides for determining the usefulness of original materials for further study and research.

While the articles abstracted here span a period of some forty years, dating as early as 1928 and as recent as 1969, by far the greater part derives from periodical scholarship of the 1950's and 60's, two decades that produced the remarkable surge of Melville criticism that continues unabated today. The number of abstracts assigned each individual work was determined by what the editors judged to be the relative importance of that work in the Melville canon and by the amount and kind of critical attention it has received; the arrangement of materials follows that principle. For internal consistency and to provide an overview of developing critical attitudes on individual works, each set of abstracts is arranged chronologically in order of publication of the original articles. From the wealth of material available, the many excellent articles not selected for abstract and presentation were excluded not out of bias or ignorance, but rather because those included better fit the demands of what is intended to be a balanced and representative collection.

We sincerely acknowledge the combined efforts of Richard Welna, David R. Lett, and Paula Fitzpatrick of Scott, Foresman in the preparation of this text. Thanks are also due James A. Hamby for his help in preparing the manuscript.

James K. Bowen
Richard VanDerBeets

Contents

Herman Melville

(1819-1891)

Born in New York City in 1819 of a Unitarian father and a Calvinist mother of the Dutch Reformed Church, Herman Melville enjoyed a childhood amid the comforts and security of a relatively well-to-do family. However, in 1832 the untimely death of his father, who had by then gone into bankruptcy, left the family subject to the munificence of kind relatives and the assistance of charitable friends. Although it is a matter of biographical conjecture as to how large a part this early traumatic experience and the subsequent disappointing adolescence played in young Melville's decision to ship before the mast as a seaman, it is a matter of critical and narrative record that his sea wanderings were creatively translated and expressed in much of his fiction. For example, just as Melville's first voyage aboard the merchant ship *St. Lawrence,* bound for Liverpool, provided much of the creative ground for *Redburn* (1849), his subsequent voyage on the *Acushnet,* a whaler out of New Bedford and bound for the South Seas, gave Melville much in the way of romantic background for his novels *Typee* (1846) and *Omoo* (1847).

But Melville is much more than a storyteller of adventure on the high seas and on exotic islands; indeed, his highly rewarding personal associations with men such as Nathaniel Hawthorne and his careful and perceptive reading of Shakespeare, Sir Thomas Browne, and Carlyle were instrumental in carrying him beyond romance to the soundings of his own inner depths. Questioning the circumstances of man cast loose from traditional religious, political, and philosophical moorings and caught in the maze of human existence, Melville penetrated the masks of appearance and illusion and in the process wrote what is considered one of the major novels of all times, *Moby-Dick* (1851).

Unfortunately for Melville, this shift from an emphasis on romantic adventure to an emphasis on metaphysics did not bring him commensurate financial and critical reward. Like so many artists who live out of their own time, he found that by not accommodating the popular tastes, which demanded less thought and more action, his audience dwindled. Although he attempted to return to his earlier mode of writing as evidenced by *Israel Potter* (1855), he could not produce the type of novel that had brought him his early acclaim. After publishing *The Piazza Tales* (1856) and *The Confidence-Man* (1857), he was forced to take a job as a customs inspector in New York in 1866 in order to provide for his wife and children. During this time he wrote two volumes of poetry, *Battle Pieces and Aspects of the War* (1866) and *Clarel* (1867); however, he remained in the literary limbo of oblivion, a condition which maintained for years after his death in 1891. Even the perceptive Henry James, as late as 1898, saw Melville as a man whose prose was "as mild and as easy as an Indian summer in the woods" and grouped him with the now-forgotten writers, George William Curtis and "Ik Marvel."

Fortunately, this particular assessment was not a lasting one. Men like Raymond Weaver and D. H. Lawrence, along with a growing number of readers and critics on both sides of the Atlantic, which included Viola Meynell, H. M. Tomlinson, Lewis Mumford, Frank Jewett Mather, and Lincoln Colcord, began to find Melville the fascinating writer that he is. And as the abstracts and bibliography in this volume attest, interest in Melville grows each year. Approaching Melville from as many points as one finds on the compass, critical analysis continues to discover new and exciting currents and undercurrents running through almost everything that he wrote.

GENERAL

Frederic I. Carpenter
MELVILLE: THE WORLD IN A MAN-OF-WAR
UKCR, XIX (Summer 1953), 257-264

Although he believed in the democratic ideal, Melville nevertheless felt it was doomed to failure. In prophesying the failure of the democratic ideal, which attempts politically to achieve the Christian goal of the brotherhood of man, Melville rejected the tenets of Protestant Christianity, a major source of American idealism, and placed himself on the side of traditional orthodox Christianity, which denies the hope of realizing the Christian ideal in this world. In the ideal realm, Melville empathized with the libertarian democrat, but in the actual realm he supported the adherence to authoritarian laws. In all Melville's novels there is implied a criticism of the democratic ideal. *Moby-Dick* is an allegory of democracy. The captain is a democratic leader of a crew who have signed on voluntarily. The crew are persuaded to give up their democratic rights in the pursuit of profit and the war against evil, and the result is disaster. The novel thus allegorizes two inherent dangers of democracy: the possibility that men may voluntarily surrender their freedoms and the threat that they may mix their dream of democracy with the romantic dream of world dominion. Thus in *Moby-Dick* Melville prophesies the doom of democracy. The crew of the *Pequod* voluntarily surrender their rights and embrace an evil goal in a time of peace. The setting of *Billy Budd* is war time when martial law must prevail. In this story Melville justifies man's eternal inhumanity to man and denies the responsibility of man for the laws which he himself has made. Here, man's first duty is to his king, his second to his God.

William Van O'Connor
MELVILLE ON THE NATURE OF HOPE
UKCR, XXII (Winter 1955), 123-130

Many of Melville's stories are philosophical explorations into the nature of hope and despair. Between 1852, when he wrote *Pierre,* and 1857, the date of *The Confidence-Man,* Melville was particularly concerned with romantic innocence and hope. In *Pierre,* he probes the nature of innocence, in which a narrow adherence to virtuousness leads to destruction. The theme underlying the novel is expressed in Plinlimmon's tract on "chronometrical" and "horological" time. Plinlimmon points out that human beings, imperfect and unangelic, who try to adhere rigidly "to the highest abstract heavenly righteousness" are doomed to failure. This attitude does not deny horror but serves to control it by encouraging man to probe deeply into his own heart and acknowledge the extremes of darkness and light within himself. Through his rigid adherence to an absolute of virtuousness, Pierre arrives at psychoneurosis and ends by destroying himself and his loved ones. Several stories in *The Piazza Tales* (1856) concern the theme of failure and frustration. "Cock-A-Doodle-Do!" demonstrates the idea that excessive hope may be destructive. "Jimmy Rose," on the other hand, stresses the idea that hope is necessary for human survival. "Benito Cereno" contrasts the hopefulness of Captain Delano with the despair of Benito Cereno. The American captain represents the innocence, ignorance, and irresponsibility of those Americans who could not foresee the dangers of slavery. In *The Confidence-Man* more than just a satire of optimism and hope is presented, for ultimately the novel suggests that charity, or faith in Providence, is necessary, so long as one does not deceive himself, that one must make preparations against disaster, without the total lack of faith which creates apprehensiveness.

Ray B. West, Jr.
PRIMITIVISM IN MELVILLE
PrS, XXX (Winter 1956), 369-385

Melville saw the crisis of Christendom in terms of a conflict between an allegiance to nature, which in its extreme form had resulted in the excesses of the French Revolution, and an allegiance to monarchy, which in its extreme form had resulted in the oppressiveness and injustice of monarchical rule. The French Revolution was a case of the extreme of uncontrolled barbarism in conflict with the extreme of a decadent society and its stifling order. Melville felt the solution to such conflict lay in a rebirth of the conventional forms of society through natural virtue, as exemplified in the primitive innocence of Billy Budd. He compares primitivism and civilization in *Moby-Dick,* but his comparison is more complex than that of his earlier novels. In *Moby-Dick* he shows the values and limitations of both primitive and civilized societies. The primitive is seen as both a revivifying force and a source of evil. Qualities associated with the savage include intuitive behavior, spontaneity, action, and colorfulness while those associated with Western man include intellect, reason, and courage.

The primitive possesses the attributes of life and nature which enable man to act. The task of the intellect is to check such energy and turn it towards rational, reasonable ends. Ahab is dehumanized when he forgets the reasonable goals of his voyage and becomes obsessed with revenge. In *Moby-Dick,* evil and innocence are closely related, and the tragic hero suffers for his attempt to return to his primitive beginnings and to view the world only in terms of action and instinct. But in *Billy Budd,* primitive innocence atones for evil through its sacrifice and thus serves as a revivifying force for a dying society.

Milton R. Stern

SOME TECHNIQUES OF MELVILLE'S PERCEPTION

*PMLA,*LXXIII (June 1958), 251-259

Melville attacks romanticism and develops a naturalistic world view with four techniques, which derive from romantic symbolism, not naturalism. All four test reality in terms of experience, not theory, and find transcendental perception a delusion. *Reinforcement* intensifies concrete, historical definitions through repetition; it undercuts ideal, cosmic absolutes with vulgar realities; man must depend on man (not on his idealized projections). *Contrast* defines reality in terms of relations, ambiguities, and limitations, not transcendental equations and infinite possibilities. *Multiple view* further develops relativity and limitation; it tests reality through diverse viewpoints, subjectively, yet denies whole truth to any individual ("The Doubloon" belies Emerson). Limited man sees only nature's surfaces; when he creates cosmic symbols from limited data, mistakes his own projections for ultimate reality, warps history to fit theory, and submits to his own idols, he destroys the heart. This is not devoutness but monomania, madness, and blasphemy. But once he accepts limitation, turns from ungraspable nature to man, and acknowledges brotherhood and love, he can become divinely noble. *Circular reflection* relates a single cluster of symbols to elements beyond its immediate scope. With all elements in tension, this technique interprets reality in terms of their context, use, and relationships; it works inductively through operational definitions to emphasize the process of relative definition, and discovers meaning through interactions (not absolute equations). Thus Melville forces a reevaluation of American naturalism; since he and Emerson both seek reality in symbolism, naturalism and romanticism need not be seen as totally estranged in their aims and instruments.

James E. Miller, Jr.
THE COMPLEX FIGURE IN MELVILLE'S CARPET
ArQ., XV (1959), 197-210

Like the "complex figure in a Persian carpet" referred to in Henry James' "The Figure in the Carpet," one major theme runs through the Melville canon. This is the idea that man must compromise with his ideals so that he can come to terms with the evil in himself and in the universe. The usual response to evil in Melville's world is to assume a mask of innocence. Melville's "masked" characters fall into two groups: those who wear masks to disguise an iniquitous intent and those who unconsciously wear masks and mistakenly assume them to be their real faces. The degree of evil produced has little or no relationship to the extent of the character's awareness of his mask, for the greatest evil could result from the most apparently innocent, as is the case for example in *Billy Budd.* Maskless men also appear in Melville's books, men who are nakedly exposed and, ironically, whose greatest claim to innocence derives from their making no pretense to having it. In between these two types are the seekers and wanderers who must choose whether or not to wear the mask of innocence. Melville's masked men include Taji, Ahab, Pierre, Bartleby, Benito Cereno, the Confidence-Man, and Billy Budd. His maskless men include Babbalanja (*Mardi*), Ishmael and Bulkington (*Moby-Dick*), Plinlimmon (*Pierre*), Winsome and Egbert (*The Confidence-Man*), and Israel Potter. In between are those characters who decide to shed their masks of innocence and accept both their involvement and the burden of guilt which accompanies the human condition. Thus baptized into humanity are Redburn, White-Jacket, Clarel, and Captain Vere.

Richard B. Sewall
AHAB'S QUENCHLESS FEUD: THE TRAGIC VISION IN SHAKESPEARE AND MELVILLE
CD, I (Fall 1967), 207-218

The question of *involvement* is a precarious one in literary discussion. Is *Moby-Dick* a document in Melville's personal "quarrel with God"? Do Shakespeare's great tragedies in any way embody his own spiritual turbulence? And what about the involvement of *us*, the audience? From Melville's *obiter dicta* and from the comments of friends (like Hawthorne) about him, it seems clear that "Ahab's quenchless feud" was in some degree his own. Melville praised Hawthorne as being the only one of his contemporaries to deal with the "tragic phase" of humanity and followed him into the tragic lists himself with *Moby-Dick*. Did Shakespeare similarly, about 1600, enter the tragic lists and, consciously, perhaps for purposes not dissimilar to Melville's, adopt the grim logic of the tragic form? Both writers had apprenticeships involving them in experiments in many modes. Shakespeare's comedies and histories reveal a gradual sharpening of focus on the plight of the individual, finally the "ever-burdened individual" facing the cosmic questions of the major tragedies. The terms of "Ahab's quenchless feud" seem everywhere applicable, especially in *Lear*. In short: we know a great deal about Melville, little about Shakespeare. Extrapolation from one to the other is admittedly dangerous. To assert their not unlikely kinship is to recognize their partnership in a common enterprise that began with the Greeks and extends at least to Faulkner. To study both authors in this perspective is to become aware of certain massive, archetypal purposes, functions, and norms. The old atavisms stir again. "Ahab's quenchless feud" was in part Melville's; in part Shakespeare's, although he made more of it; it is in part *ours*, although we must make still more of it if we are to survive. Such is the universal involvement that tragedy seems everywhere to demand.*

B. L. Reid

OLD MELVILLE'S FABLE

Mass R, I X (Summer 1968), 529-546

Moby-Dick and *Billy Budd* are the poles of a lifetime's theological argument. In *Billy Budd* the subject is again tragic destiny, fall of man with loss of Eden, but in old age Melville has learned a new way to tell a tragic story: *Billy Budd* is the classical answer to *Moby-Dick's* romantic cry. With his speaking voice under control for the first time, Melville achieves the grandsire tone of an ideal myth-maker, of a collective racial intelligence: committed but speculative, philosophic but pragmatical, ruminative, knowing, weary but not exhausted, heartbroken but forgiving. This narrative voice controls the order and proportion of elements to create, by means of complex stylization, a homiletic legend fabular and representative. Out of a realistic tale enriched by the whole available store of human typology—history, legend, literature, Christian and pagan myth—Melville makes not an allegory but a symbolic fable. Character and action use and extend the visions of Milton and Hawthorne: innocence strikes back at evil and is terribly punished by a mediating judge, a necessitarian, a good man who is powerless to prevent a tragedy of injustice. By the dignity of his persons and of his narrative invention and control, in legend not drama, Melville makes literary tragedy out of folk tragedy. The story's logic does not accept the rightness of tragic destiny as exemplified by Billy's purity, Claggart's wickedness, and Vere's helplessness; but the story's art accepts and celebrates the symmetry of necessity, the comeliness of the terrible mystery.*

MOBY-DICK

(1851)

Charles C. Walcutt

THE FIRE SYMBOLISM IN MOBY-DICK

MLN, LIX (1944), 304-310

There is a crucial passage near the end of *Moby-Dick* in which Ahab seizes the links of the lightning chain, puts his foot upon Fedallah's body, and speaks to the St. Elmo's fire burning off the ends of the spars. Here he refers to himself as a Persian fire-worshipper who received his scar by burning, and he affirms his devotion to the "clear spirit of clear fire" which has "unconditional, unintegral mastery" in him. This passage is the key to the many confusing and paradoxical references in the novel to fire. Zoroastrianism holds that the universe is divided by a conflict between good and evil. Fedallah, Ahab's alter ego, is a Mephistopheles who has seduced Ahab into selling his soul to him for assistance in trapping the whale. He is also, as a Parsee, a fire-worshipper, and his presence suggests that Ahab has practiced Zoroastrianism with his assistance. In Zoroastrianism fire represents good. Why, then, the association in the novel of fire with evil? Ahab evolves in the course of the story. Before the novel opens, he presumably subscribes to the Christian belief in God's goodness and omnipotence. But experience and reflection make him recognize the overpowering presence of evil in the universe. He gradually sees that evil cannot be conquered but that man can rise to greatness through his tragic struggle with evil. Good and evil are not separate forces in the universe but are fused into One. The fire symbolism in the novel supports this idea. Ahab first worships fire as the destroyer of evil. As he matures in wisdom, however, he recognizes the fusion of opposites in the universe. In this passage, then, Ahab identifies himself with the fire and admits his membership in the order of nature. He cannot rest content with this wisdom, however, but must proceed to self-destruction; like the Phoenix, he must be purified through fire.

R. W. Short
MELVILLE AS SYMBOLIST
UKCR, XV (1948), 38-46

Moby-Dick is not allegorical in the way that the works of Hawthorne, Dante, or Bunyan are. Strict allegory deals with experience which has passed through doctrine into dogma, and Melville was opposed to dogma because he felt in its narrowness it failed to provide a full account of experience. Melville is concerned with getting at the realities behind the "pasteboard masks." His treatment of physical objects thus emphasizes the concrete aspects of reality; but what these things represent, their subsurface realities, reach us indirectly, through the concrete. His treatment of persons is just the opposite, for he presents fantastic, exotic characters against plain, concrete backdrops. He wanted his characters to be originals, in the mold of Adam, Eve, and Satan. Like Shakespeare, Melville needed to create a myth-world where the laws of probability could be relaxed, enabling him to get at the experience behind the dark glass of reality. Only the objects are real in *Moby-Dick,* not the people. Unlike Shakespeare, who was able to people his myth-world with real persons, Melville presented only the concrete reality of physical objects, not real people grappling with ultimate values. Melville's symbols blur into one another. Moby-Dick is an archetypal symbol containing within himself all possibilities. He is evil, considered from a human viewpoint, yet he is also God. Melville thus repudiated the Puritan belief in the separation of good and evil, while maintaining the Calvinistic stress upon the latter.

Donald Weeks
TWO USES OF MOBY-DICK
AQ, II (Summer 1950), 155-164

Moby-Dick functions in two ways: as art and as moral discourse, the one revealing what fiction may do, the other what men may do and what it is to suffer. All too prone to pigeonhole fiction into neat genres, nineteenth- and twentieth-century critics were unprepared to judge *Moby-Dick's* eclectic art relative to its overall effect. For us, the novel is a revenge tragedy. Unlike a dramatist, a novelist can oppose action with weighty thoughts. In *Moby-Dick* three themes oppose Ahab's tragic revenge. The first is the theme of cetology which fleshes out otherwise will-o'-the-wisp symbols and contributes to the terror of Ahab's death. Delight, dignity, and peace form the second counterbalance to Ahab. The third is the fellowship theme, proceeding from the monkey rope and gams to Ahab's recognition of interdebtedness. These three artistic touchstones—defining the good—question Ahab's evil purpose. They prepare us for Ahab's fall and for a moral catharsis still relevant today, for *Moby-Dick* is about dictatorship. Though some critics find Ahab morally great in his rebellion, Melville tells us that Ahab is blind and mad and his death a mean, impersonal act of fate. He is determinedly evil, and the catharsis comes as we see him triumphant over impotent good. Responsibility fails against such iniquity, now as then; even Ishmael accepts Ahab's tyranny passively. Thus like Shakespeare in *King Lear,* Melville undergirds his metaphysics with particular reality, and as a part of this art he uses strong moral examples of iniquity.

Henry A. Murray
IN NOMINE DIABOLI
NEQ, XXIV (December 1951), 435-452

In *Moby-Dick* Melville displays myth-making powers worthy of a Blake. Ahab embodies an archetypal Lucifer, the Fallen Angel. To the Church Fathers he would have been "anti-Christ," not Satan himself, but a human being with his energy and pride. One cannot doubt that Melville intended to mold Ahab after Satan, for he told Hawthorne that his novel had been boiled in hellfire and secretly baptized in the name of the Devil. An "ungodly, god-like" man, Ahab is beyond the realm of Christendom. He blasphemes, defies, scorns, and mocks the gods. He bears a strong resemblance to Milton's Satan, though he is depicted with greater psychological depth and insight. Excepting Starbuck, Ahab and his followers represent the primal drives forced into the unconscious mind of Western man by religion. In psychological terms, Ahab represents the id, the repressed part of the human personality while the White Whale is the superego. Ahab has projected his Calvinist conscience onto Moby-Dick, and the whale thus embodies the wrathful Old Testament God of retribution, as well as the Puritan ethic. The novel's basic conflict involves the id versus the superego, with the rational ego (Starbuck) being overcome by the fanatical id. Writing to unsettle complacent minds, Melville was like Blake's "true poet" who "is of the Devil's party." Melville realized this and thus christened his novel *In Nomine Diaboli.*

C. Merton Babcock
THE VOCABULARY OF MOBY-DICK
AS, XXVIII (1953), 91-101

When *Moby-Dick* was first published, critics heaped scorn upon Melville for his language and his literary style. In recent times, however, critics have been almost unanimous in praising both Melville's style and his language. A close examination of the words in *Moby-Dick* will reveal what Melville's actual contributions to the American and English languages have been. Melville used certain words listed as Americanisms in the *Dictionary of American English,* but his usage antedated the earliest citations given in the *DAE.* A second group of words includes those found in English before 1600 of uncertain American origin which antedate, in *Moby-Dick,* the earliest citations in the *DAE* or *A Dictionary of Americanisms.* A third group obviously constitutes Americanisms in that they appear at an earlier date than any of the citations listed in the *New English Dictionary* or its *Supplement.* Melville's priority is clearly demonstrated in a fourth group of words which are either not found in the historical dictionaries at all or are found first in Melville. He also used words which do not appear in the *NED* or *DAE* and are therefore of his own creation—nonce words, provincialisms, onomatopoetic words, or neologisms. A sixth category is comprised of words and expressions which Melville used in a different sense from those given in the historical dictionaries. Finally, several words are listed in the *NED,* drawing their historical evidence from Melville himself. Thus Melville's usage was not restricted to conventional English. *Moby-Dick* provides a kind of glossary of words originating from or peculiar to the New England whaling industry. Melville often took artistic liberties with the language as he knew it, and he demonstrated a great sensitivity to the basic elements of language formation. His contribution to the English and American languages was more through the adaptation of language to his own special purposes than through the coining of new words.

James D. Young
THE NINE GAMS OF THE PEQUOD
AL, XXV (January 1954), 449-463

The *Pequod's* gams (social meetings) with other ships reveal a sequence of basic problems in *Moby-Dick*—communication difficulties and alternative attitudes and actions with respect to the White Whale. Like Ahab, the *Pequod* is a self-sufficient microcosm of society, but it cannot escape relationship with macrocosm and thus meets nine ships. None swerves Ahab from his monomania. The first three present problems of communication: the *Albatross* of its impossibility, for the first omen of doom is that communication is inadequate at best; the *Town-Ho* of its uselessness, for the story of inhumanity punished by divine justice (whale) is kept secret from Ahab, and knowledge is not true which is not personal; the *Jereboam* of its rejection, for Ahab ignores prophetic Gabriel's warning of divine wrath against blasphemers of God (whale) and man. The next three ships present attitude problems, in the context of chapters about the whale greater than man: the *Jungfrau* shows ignorance through innocence, the *Rose-Bud* through inexperience, and the *Samuel Enderby* through indifference and rationality. The last three gams present alternatives for action: the *Bachelor* is a basis for action, paralleling Stubb's jolly, animal complacency and lack of belief; the *Rachel* presents the action itself, paralleling Starbuck's choice of man over whale (a humanity which finally saves Ishmael); the *Delight* represents the consequences of action, for it has suffered and understands the whale's destructive power and refuses further action. What each of the nine ships shows Ahab he rejects as inadequate. What they suffer makes inevitable the tragedy of the *Pequod.*

George R. Stewart
THE TWO MOBY-DICKS
AL, XXV (January 1954), 417-448

It may be theorized that Melville did not plan *Moby-Dick,* but changed its course several times. This is why he took so long to write it, found the writing frustrating, and produced a book rife with inconsistencies. Internal evidence suggests at least two versions: an original *Ur-Moby-Dick (UMD)* found almost unrevised in Chapters 1-15, and a later version

(*Moby-Dick*) found in Chapters 23 following. *UMD* was a simple sea adventure: a whale line killed hero Queequeg, and Ishmael deserted ship to a desert island. There was no Moby-Dick or *Pequod* sinking. In addition to minor details, *UMD* differs from *Moby-Dick* in major ways. Thus concepts about major characters shift: gruff Ahab becomes tragic, heroic description of Queequeg is sheer waste relative to his final role, and realistic Ishmael becomes merely Melville's voice. The prosy, colloquial *UMD* style becomes conventionally poetic. Shakespearean allusions are slight in Chapters 1–15 but major later. The *UMD* atmosphere, realistic and even folksy, becomes epic, grand, and tragic in *Moby-Dick* as Melville engages in philosophical, otherworldly allegory. And the name significances of many characters lose their appropriateness in the final version. Though the partly revised Transition, Chapters 16–22, splices *UMD* with the following chapters (introducing tragic Ahab and the strange *Pequod* and foreshadowing Fedallah and mystery), there are hardly any details in *UMD* which relate organically to *Moby-Dick*. The contrast between realistic *UMD* and allegorical *Moby-Dick*, doubtless due to the pressure under which Melville worked, reveals his failure to make the two versions harmonious.

John Parke

SEVEN MOBY-DICKS

NEQ, XXVIII (September 1955), 319-338

Moby-Dick is an exciting tale of physical adventure, depicting the struggle between man and nature and the effect each has on the other. It is also a moral drama of the struggle within the soul of man, a many-layered allegory interpretable on at least seven levels. Melville's universe is indifferent, impersonal, and neutral toward man, and thus man's view of it as malevolent or benevolent is merely a projection of his own inner state of being. Ahab's malevolent world is only a projection of his own inner torment. He succumbs to *hubris* in his attack on nature, and unlike Starbuck, the only whole, totally human man on the *Pequod,* is unbalanced and inhuman. He is a prideful renegade seeking complete dominance over circumstance, but although a renegade outside the realm of Christendom, still he dies a hero. Like Prometheus, in his refusal to accept a fate which he cannot comprehend or control, Ahab is a tragic hero who realizes the extent of his sacrifice in seeking to overcome fate. He dies unrepentant in an uncaring, purposeless universe empty of God. However, his confrontation with metaphysical chaos gives him epic greatness. Melville suggests that the evil within man produces external chaos in the universe. Ultimately, the novel is an examination of evil. Ahab is an archetypal hero, who, in battling evil, discovers its existence within himself, and his tragedy lies in his persistent struggle against and inability to deal with this force. For Melville would have us see that all of man's attempts to deny or resist evil are futile, since it is part of him and must be dealt with.

J. A. Ward

THE FUNCTION OF THE CETOLOGICAL CHAPTERS IN MOBY-DICK

AL, XXVIII (May 1956), 164-183

Melville's whale-and-whaling chapters give the voyage epic duration and variety, expand characters' proportions, and educate the public about whaling so that the narrative, its factual basis established, may dramatically intensify and accelerate. While stable whaling facts anchor metaphysics to earth, making fantasy credible, mock-heroic burlesque ridicules the scientific approach, undercutting any pretense that facts alone can soar beyond earth. The primary quest in the cetological chapters is knowledge, with relatedness the key to knowledge and symbolism the approach. Thus to know one thing fully is to know the universe—the whale links all worlds. Symbolism transforms the concrete facts of the universe into metaphysics; the whale reconciles opposites (physical revealing spiritual realities) and unifies knowledge (approached through science, legend, art, history, literature, religion). Like Shakespeare, Melville never allows any single viewpoint to dominate; knowledge comes through mutual tension between subjectivism (dangerously narrow), transcendentalism (seeing false subsurface realities), and science (seeing surfaces alone, the whole merely an abstraction of parts). Neither reason (Locke) nor understanding (Kant) fathoms relationships and ambiguities. Only symbolism (with metaphor, analogy, allusion) is comprehensive; this method, developed in *Typee* and *White-Jacket,* Melville brings to fullness in *Moby-Dick.* It builds from a concrete inductive frame to metaphysics and myth, reflecting life's essential relatedness. The whale, its depth-reality as inscrutable as its surface appearance, can never be known completely. But symbolism sounds the depths.

Otis Wheeler
HUMOR IN MOBY-DICK: TWO PROBLEMS
AL, XXIX (May 1957), 203-206

Despite recent scholarship on humor in *Moby-Dick,* two problems remain. First, Ishmael values humor early but later values sorrow. Second, the comedy-team role passes from Ishmael-Queequeg to Stubb-Flask. George R. Stewart's "The Two *Moby-Dicks*" offers a solution: an early *Moby-Dick* about Queequeg and narrator-Ishmael (Chapters 1-15) was grafted onto the later Ahab story (Chapters 23 following); the book remains disjointed. Thus a bumptious Ishmael narrates the first part and in Chapter 5 values jolly laughter, but it is a pessimistic, philosophical narrator in Chapter 96 who calls a soul undeveloped which has more joy than sorrow. When Melville rethought *Moby-Dick,* his early concept of Ishmael did not fit, but he hated to scrap his first several chapters (perhaps already set in galley). Thus Ishmael's light-hearted viewpoint shifts (or even disappears, replaced by an omniscient author) to support Ahab's tragic character and to suit grim interior monologues. This shift solves the second problem. Since the *Pequod* is a microcosm of life, a high-spirited comic element is necessary, for it is just as much a part of life as Ahab's tragedy (which it defines by contrast). But comic Ishmael is gone, because no such skylarking narrator could possibly fathom tragedy, and so the funnyman role goes to Stubb, with Flask his straight man (Queequeg, Ishmael's bloodbrother, could hardly play opposite Stubb). Thus the comic role passes from Ishmael and Queequeg as their jocularity and cannibal humor give way to larger, more sublime themes. Though this shift splits *Moby-Dick* structurally, it enhances its tragic grandeur which is more to be valued than flawless technique.

Dan Vogel
THE DRAMATIC CHAPTERS IN MOBY-DICK
NCF, XIII (December 1958), 239-247

Moby-Dick contains two dramas: the conflict between Ahab and the whale and the conflict between Ahab and his crew. Melville stages the human drama aboard the *Pequod* in thirteen chapters, complete with stage settings, stage directions, and soliloquies. In this section Melville dispenses with his regular narrative point of view in order to stage the conflict of his characters. His use of auctorial characterization before his protagonists engage in dialogue is a dramatist's technique. These chapters are linked by the use of stage directions. The Exposition includes Chapter 29 (Ahab vs. Stubb); the Rising Action includes Chapters 36 through 40 (Ahab vs. Starbuck, Ahab's soliloquy, Starbuck's resolution, Stubb's retreat, and the introduction of Pip); Chapter 108 comprises the Interlude (Ahab and the carpenter); the Climax includes Chapters 119 through 122 (Ahab vs. Starbuck, Starbuck's resignation, Stubb's resignation, Tashtego's attitude); and the Falling Action and Catharsis include Chapters 127 through 129 (Ahab vs. Pip, Pip's resignation). By beginning his drama with Stubb, Melville is able to expound the intent of the dramatic chapters, make Stubb a foil to Starbuck, and prepare the way for Ahab's greater conflict with Starbuck. There are soliloquies in Chapters 37 and 38. Chapter 40 allows a broadening of the ranks of men to include the whole crew, thus completing the microcosm and defining the fear which galvanizes the conflict of character. Chapter 108 seems to have been derived from the porter scene in *Macbeth,* while Ahab's relationship with Pip seems to have been derived from that of King Lear and his fool. The Falling Action shows Pip's humanizing influence on Ahab and his madness which is close to truth. In keeping with this foregoing dramatic action, Ahab is proceeding to the inevitable catastrophe when the curtain descends on the last of the dramatic chapters.

Curtis Dahl
MOBY-DICK'S COUSIN BEHEMOTH
AL, XXXI (March 1959), 21-29

Melville knew Cornelius Mathews' popular *Behemoth: A Legend of the Mound-Builders* (1839), which strikingly foreshadows Moby-Dick and Ahab. Hero Bokulla suffers defeats but finally kills Behemoth, the primeval mastodon which ravaged his American tribe. Like Moby-Dick, Behemoth is huge and supernatural—immortal, invulnerable—his tremendous physical power matched by malign instinct. His power rivals God's. A barbaric idol the people both fear and worship, he is morally ambiguous, a paralyzing, spiritual terror with flaming eyes, yet calm and sublime. Swimming alone in the sea, he is an island of Eternal Quiet, innocently spouting rainbows. Mathews allegorizes Behemoth with mythical allusions, yet his Titan lacks Melville's ambiguity (of aspiration-blasphemy). Like Ahab, Bokulla is solitary and epic, and as both fiend and angel, he is morally ambiguous. Shameful defeat rouses him from darkness to passionate, courageous action, and his physical quest becomes metaphysical; in his monomania (but without Ahab's blasphemy) he fights to prove man's will triumphant over bestiality. Other parallels occur: weapons preparation, epic rhetoric, some humor, a fatality theme, allusions (to Bible, Classics, American tales). Primarily, both authors make physical monsters spiritual manifestations of nature's inherent (Manichaean) evil. Yet Mathews is no Melville. He fails to develop secondary characters, allegory, allusions, and ambiguities; suspense comes through actions, not ideas; morality and reality remain unfathomed. In contrast, Melville is intensely artistic, comprehensive, and profoundly deep.

Charles H. Foster
SOMETHING IN EMBLEMS: A REINTERPRETATION OF MOBY-DICK
NEQ, XXXIV (March 1961), 3-35

Moby-Dick is not two books—a picaresque sea story and a later Shakespearean tragedy—but three. In 1851 it became a radically democratic fable attacking slavery. Slavery spurred the rewrite, not conservative Hawthorne, for Melville was conservative in no sense. The Sims case of 1851 angered him. A fugitive Negro, Sims was brutally remanded to Georgia under the Fugitive Slave Act (1850) by Chief Justice Lemuel Shaw, Melville's father-in-law. Shaw installed a chain around the courthouse and had to pass under it himself, his genuflexion metaphorically *something in emblems*. Hawthorne supported both Shaw and President Pierce against radicals who would tear apart the Constitution (with its pro-slavery clauses) and nation. Melville warned Hawthorne that *Moby-Dick* would be uncompromisingly, dangerously radical; he rewrote the tragedy, infusing it with revolutionary attitudes. Attacking conservatives, Father Mapple's Sermon is similar to contemporary radical speeches: Heaven's Patriots, pluck out the government's sins!—Never compromise God's laws with man's (Constitution included)! A prayer (Chapter 26) defies Shaw, underscoring democracy's God-ordained equality. "The Town-Ho's Story" advocates mutiny against tyranny; divine Moby-Dick destroys arbitrary authority. Pip cries mercy from white-god Ahab; Ahab-Shaw turns on his Sims. Yet Ahab is mainly Daniel Webster—devil-baptized, demagogic, and tragic, and his fire worship echoes Webster's advocacy of northern industrialism. With Ahab-Webster guiding, the whole ship-state participates in guilt—and disaster. Moby-Dick symbolizes nature offended, not offending. Civilized and Christian, Melville fought slavery's blasphemy tooth and whale.

H. C. Brashers
ISHMAEL'S TATTOOS
SR, LXX (Winter 1962) 137-154

In *Moby Dick* Melville presents the problem of how man may achieve psychic balance in his relationship with the universe. By the end of the novel the introspective and reflective Ishmael, with the aid of Queequeg's instinct, achieves a delicate balance of feeling and judgment. He unconsciously learns the lessons of Queequeg's tattoos, containing a "complete theory of the heavens and the earth, a mystical treatise on the art of attaining truth." This lesson is psychically "tattooed" on Ishmael's soul. Ishmael and Queequeg are character foils to Ahab, with Queequeg unconsciously teaching Ishmael how to attain the truth and evaluate experience, and showing him where to place himself in the universe. A man of feeling, Queequeg instinctively dramatizes the lesson of his tattoos. Ahab represents the Old Testament negative morality of "Thou shalt not." The New Testament ethic is love, a positive attitude, but mankind has been reared on morals and cannot make the leap to the positive ethic of love. Ishmael evolves from a man lacking self-identity and suffering from a feeling of chaos and a lack of kinship with the universe to a man who learns to practice the Golden Rule and follow the truths of the heart. Queequeg teaches him to be tolerant, to live one's religion, and to achieve the delicate balance between one's individual identity and the identity resulting from kinship with all creatures of the universe. Ahab's identity is egomaniacal and destructive, allied with the "Thou-shalt-not" morality. Ishmael sees the dangers of submersion in transcendentalism and submission to religious mania. He even develops a negative capability, the ability to accept reality without intellectualizing it, which sustains his psychic balance at the end when he is knocked overboard. He thus achieves both a literal and a symbolic salvation and is the one character who is able to achieve a positive view of life based on the ethical lesson of Queequeg's tattoos.

Allen Austin
THE THREE-STRANDED ALLEGORY OF MOBY-DICK
CE, XXVI (February 1965), 344-349

Death (Moby-Dick) cancels all hope of immortality. Based on Ahab's supernaturalism and Ishmael's opposing atheism, three strands of allegory develop this central theme. First, Melville satirizes transcendentalism and individualism. As Ahab personifies impersonal nature he becomes transcendental and mad; like Narcissus, he seeks revenge against his own self-projection. Though admirably defiant, Ahab in his individualism fails to recognize man's dependence on his fellows or to accept responsibility for anyone but himself. Melville satirizes this Emersonian self-reliance and advocates fellowship, for society is a joint-stock company of mutual responsibility. Second, Melville satirizes Christianity. Mad Ahab justly defies Christian doctrine which calls the universal destroyer a God of Love; with anger and woe, atheistic Ishmael sees only death in Moby-Dick and defies Christian faith. Discontent with facts, Christians invert evil into false good and conjure their dream of immortality: woe, madness, and horror are truer than Starbuck's outrageous illusions. Third, Melville advocates a naturalistic, pessimistic philosophy. As the *Pequod* sinks and a coffin saves Ishmael, he becomes Christ (replacing Fedallah-Christ), yet Ishmael (no Spirit-child Isaac) is a mortal and refutes the gospel. Like Job's messengers, he bears tidings of death, evil news of orphaned man chasing illusions in a savage, indifferent universe. If the doubloon signifies anything, it is that each man may interpret its appearance as he likes—but its only reality is impersonality, emptiness, and death.

Jerome Ellison
HOW TO CATCH A WHALE
MQR, VI (Spring 1967), 85-89

Modern critics have preferred descriptive analysis to evaluations, thus eschewing questions of good and evil. Consequently, some of us propose an approach we call "Evolutionary" criticism. *Moby-Dick* provides illustrations of the issues involved. The good-and-evil theme is of such dimension that it cannot be contained by any concept that does not bring within its view the entire experience of man on earth. The twentieth-century name for this experience is evolution-of-consciousness

(Julian Huxley, 1942; P.B. Medawar, 1960). Man's *consciousness* is evolving; evidence is found in the stories of those writers who have made myths. We are modern men with the caveman's mind stuffed into the unconscious, from whence it conducts a relentless campaign to regain ground from consciousness. C.G. Jung assigns to literature a central role in our psychorevolutionary advance. The agonized work goes on, with writers as both participants and observers. Because of its powerful laying bare of these mechanics, Jung considered *Moby-Dick* America's greatest novel. Evolutionary criticism would rank the book high. That which advances consciousness, extends and sharpens awareness (Ishmael-Starbuck), is good. That ever-present undertow, tending to pull us back to the primitive, unreflective mire (Moby-Dick-Ahab), is evil.*

Herbert G. Eldridge
"CAREFUL DISORDER": THE STRUCTURE
OF MOBY-DICK
AL, XXXIX (May 1967), 145-162

In respect to the structure of *Moby-Dick,* critics have either compared the novel to plays and epic poems or have decided that no controlling arrangement is discernible. However, there is evidence that Melville developed the novel from an outline, maintaining a general symmetry, despite the "organic" addition of chapters or groups of chapters, and using patterns he had tested in *Redburn* and *White-Jacket.* The primary divisions after the New Bedford-Nantucket unit of 22 chapters are the oceanic segments of the voyage—Atlantic (28 chapters), Indian (36), Java-China (24), Pacific (19) and "On-the-line" (6), transitions being marked by unique chapters offering geographical facts and dramatic emphasis. Moreover, each of the six voyage blocks contains evidence of further division at its centerpoint in the numerical sequence of chapters, indicated by style, technique, episode, and theme—for example, the soliloquy-gam sets at the middle of the Indian and Java-China segments and Ahab's histrionic violence at the center of the Atlantic and Pacific units. In fact, these repetitions suggest an arrangement of balanced pairs, the story moving from point to point around a structural hexagon, with "Loomings" and the Epilogue closing the figure. Finally, the six-part scheme partitions the novel logically in respect to Melville's major fictional problems, such as establishing point of view (New Bedford—Nantucket) and introducing *dramatis personae* and cetology (Atlantic). In chapter LXXXII, Melville praises "careful disorderliness" as a fictional method; we can see that the "organic disorder" of *Moby-Dick* was supported by the architecture necessary for orderly growth.*

Allan and Barbara Lefcowitz
AHAB'S OTHER LEG: NOTES ON MELVILLE'S SYMBOLIC METHOD
ESQ, XLVII (II Quarter 1967), 23-27

Melville's symbolic methodology in *Moby-Dick,* as revealed through the perceptions of Ishmael, encompasses the following phases: (a) *imaginative prefiguration;* vague, inchoate suppositions about the ontology of an object or person, (b) reinforcement through first-hand *sense impressions* of the facts; limited analysis, (c) passage of *time,* in which there may occur the use of antithesis or contrast, (d) return to "the facts"; pragmatic testing; *verification,* (e) expansion; enrichment; final *synthesis.* The symbolic development of Ahab's ivory leg illustrates the progression. During the early chapters, the leg operates either on a literal level (supporting Ahab and causing wonder and fear in his crew), or as an emblem for natural malevolence as well as a rationale for revenge. During the middle chapters, the leg is physically present to the consciousness as its sound reminds the crew that Ahab is omnipresent. In the last chapters, the leg must be replaced, and in the process it is converted into a richly complex symbol suggesting the nature of man as a *bricoleur* whose universe is already closed to further effort (though not to rearrangement); the paradoxical dependence of spirit on matter; and the very nature of man as a shaper of matter in symbol. This process is connected to Ishmael by means of another material creation of the carpenter—the coffin–sea chest-life buoy—which is analogous to the leg since the coffin is at once the material support for the symbol maker, Ishmael, and the material for his symbolic processes. The way to grasp Melville's symbols, then, is to grasp both the genesis of the fact and the "perceptual abilities of the omnisentient mind of the symbol-maker as well," keeping in mind that the catalyst in the process is time.*

William B. Dillingham

THE NARRATOR OF MOBY-DICK

ES, XLIX (February 1968), 20-29

The tone of *Moby-Dick* was described by early reviewers as strange and "wild." That tone, which is in many places much like the humor that the mad or the half-mad create, can be attributed largely to the state of mind of Ishmael, the narrator. When the character and role of Ishmael are clarified, the connection between tone, theme, point of view, and structure becomes clear. It is Ishmael's mind which shapes the events, his voice which articulates the ideas—in short, it is Ishmael whose presence we feel from the first page to the last. This highly sensitive, imaginative, and sometimes unstable narrator is recreating the story, both from what he actually witnessed and heard and from what he pieces together in his imagination. Ishmael is a creative narrator, whose personality and whose suffering are everywhere apparent. If the tone seems half-crazy at times it is because Ishmael is half-crazy at times. His experience aboard the *Pequod* has left him profoundly disturbed, and he retells the story of Ahab and Moby-Dick in the manner of Coleridge's Ancient Mariner. His facing of almost unendurable loneliness is basically the ordeal of Ishmael. In both works, the experience leaves the character with a burden which at times makes him all but unstable.*

Sanford Sternlicht

SERMONS IN MOBY-DICK

BSUF, X (Winter 1969), 51-52

Moby-Dick contains not one but two great sermons that prefigure the allegory and foreshadow the action of the novel as well as bundle its themes into handy sheaves. Furthermore, these sermons are juxtaposed by Melville to reflect on each other so that their mutual presence in the masterpiece offers subtle ironies for the reader. The sermons are Father Mapple's great oration in the Whaleman's Chapel of New Bedford and old Fleece's sermon to the sharks from the deck of the *Pequod.* Unlike Mapple's sermon to the sharks called men, old Fleece's sermon is ostensibly to the sharks of the sea. However, it is Fleece and not Mapple

who preaches the true sermon of life as Melville saw it, and who is chosen
by that author to state emphatically his darkly pessimistic view of man's
role and fate.*

James K. Bowen
"CRAZY AHAB" AND KIERKEGAARD'S "MELANCHOLY FANTASTIC"

RS, (March 1969), 60-64

That Ahab's anguish-filled pursuit psychologically alienates him
from his God and transports him from the actual world to the "howling
infinite" is a matter of narrative and critical record. This dive behind
"pasteboard" masks which isolates Ahab and drives him beyond the reach
and scope of his fellowmen places him directly in line with the kind of
man Soren Kierkegaard, the melancholy Dane, sees suffering from the
most far-reaching form of universal sickness endured by men who are
alienated from their creator, despair of infinitude. In Section III, Part First
of *The Sickness Unto Death,* Kierkegaard examines the circumstances and
attitudes of the man who, because of his strong imaginative prowess, is
unable to find interest in and comfort with a cipher-like existence in a
philistine world. Feeling that he can escape time's hold on him, this man
pursues a fantastical course which causes him to lose all sense of perspective. Believing all things possible, he monomaniacally plunges into the
wilderness of being, where he becomes irretrievably lost. He ignores the
complaints and pleas of those around him and eventually falls victim to
that which he simultaneously dreads and holds in awe. Comparing what
Kierkegaard does through philosophic precept with what Melville does
through creative incident, allows us to see that the intent of each writer
complements the other, and enables us to reach an understanding of both
the melancholy fantastic and crazy Ahab.*

BILLY BUDD

(1924)

E. L. G. Watson

MELVILLE'S TESTAMENT OF ACCEPTANCE

NEQ, VI (June 1933), 319-327

Although *Billy Budd* lacks the ornate language and exuberant prose which characterize *Mardi, Moby-Dick,* and *Pierre,* still it is rich, if not richer, in elaborate symbolism that is even more effective because of Melville's objective, dry style. Billy represents a kind of divine innocence unmarked by doubt, a Christ not yet aware of His own divinity who is opposed by maniacal malice. But the theme encompasses more than this. The *Indomitable* is a microcosm of the world, with threatened mutiny and war a recognized part of existence. However, rebellion is absent from this novel. Billy is too free a being to need to rebel or resist his fate. But his accepting nature arouses to action its evil opposite, and there arises a battle between unwitting virtue and the perverted, bitter nature which must destroy in order to find solace. Captain Vere also possesses this supreme quality of acceptance. He is the law-abiding man who is still able to understand the verities of the spirit. Like Pilate, he sentences the innocent man to a despicable death, but unlike him, he accepts the full responsibility for the sentence, thus taking much of the bitterness of Billy's death upon himself. Melville suggests a spiritual affinity between Vere and Billy; both seem to comprise two major elements of a greater spirit called Man. Moreover, underlying the story are shadows of a primal sexuality. Certain incidents suggesting darker depths in man's nature are undoubtedly intentional. Yet Melville only suggests, never denotes, charging his words and images with symbolic implications. Billy's last words imply his final acceptance, but more than that suggest a communion between himself and Vere, which serves to unite their two souls.

Norman Holmes Pearson

BILLY BUDD: "THE KING'S YARN"

AQ, III (Summer 1951), 99-114

Moby-Dick was a resource, if not a source, for *Billy Budd.* The original source for *Budd* was a report of the actual execution of a Midshipman Spencer for mutiny aboard the *Somers* in 1842. Spencer's technical accuser was Melville's first cousin. The full account is offered in Thurlow-Weed's autobiography of 1883. There is a striking parallel with Billy's hanging, for at the moment of execution Spencer cried, "God bless the flag!" Captain Vere also resembles Captain Mackenzie of the *Somers.* But *Budd* was drawn from many other sources as well. Material from *White-Jacket* is seen in the characters of the Dansker, Claggart, and to some extent, Billy. More than most books, however, *Budd* is filled with literary references, allusions, and analogies, and like *Moby-Dick,* the story can be most fully appreciated only by the literate. There is the apparent influence of Southey's biography of Lord Nelson. There are associations with the New Testament and with Milton, particularly concerning the concepts of original sin, fallen man, and redemption. Budd is Adam before the Fall. Claggart is Satan the Tempter. There are mythic echoes of Milton's *Paradise Lost, Paradise Regained,* and *Samson Agonistes.* Billy is also the Second Adam—Christ. Vere (*vir? veritas?*) is man after the Fall. He is also *Samson Agonistes,* for he is redeemed, and he learns how to die. Thus, like the King's yarn, that colored strand threading its way through the crown to denote royalty, Melville has threaded throughout *Billy Budd* numerous literary allusions and echoes which add depth and dimension to his tale.

Wendell Glick
EXPEDIENCY AND ABSOLUTE MORALITY IN BILLY BUDD
PMLA, LXVIII (March 1953), 103-110

In *Billy Budd,* Melville chooses social expediency over absolute morality and finds in Lord Nelson's heroism a compensating morality. Absolute morality is Christian, requiring allegiance to nature, individual justice, and humane conscience. Social expediency is utilitarian, requiring loyalty to civilization, social justice, and practical necessity; its cost is dear, especially in terms of mediocrity, but without it society would cease to exist. Mutiny threatens the British Empire, and anarchy must be avoided at all costs. Though regimentation curtails certain individual rights, anarchic chaos destroys society and all human rights. Vere pities Billy and prefers Christian morality, but he knows (like Plinlimmon) that it fails to preserve order. Billy belongs to Heaven, not earth; his hanging illustrates that absolute morality does not work in this world. Vere—representing Melville —is a realist; on the basis of his readings and experience he makes a rational, discriminating choice, sacrifices absolute morality for the higher ethic, absolute necessity, and preserves civilization. Thus, order (the *Indomitable*) triumphs over chaos (the *Athéiste*). Yet prudence (the central utilitarian ethic) produces mediocrity, and Melville seeks, instead, some possibility of an inspiring, socially vitalizing, private heroism. He finds it in Lord Nelson. Though called militarily inexpedient, Nelson's self-sacrifice at Trafalgar was expedient in the largest sense in that he inspired the British to heroism and preserved the nation. Though absolute morality is unsuited to a utilitarian world, Nelson's morality of expedient heroism offers an alternative to which man can turn.

G. Giovannini and H. M. Campbell

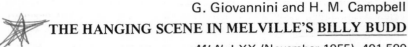 THE HANGING SCENE IN MELVILLE'S BILLY BUDD

MLN, LXX (November 1955), 491-500

Several critics have viewed the ending of *Billy Budd* ironically, maintaining that Billy achieves no salvation. Interpreting the benediction and the symbolism in the hanging scene ironically tends to oversimplify the meaning by ignoring an important dualism running throughout the story. The nihilistic pessimism of earlier works is transformed in *Billy Budd* into pessimism of another kind which is complicated by religious symbolism and transfigured by a hint of a transcendental, optimistic reality in the final scene. There is no simple conflict between optimism and pessimism, orthodoxy and unbelief, but rather a complex transcending all these. The religious symbolism supports an optimistic reading of the story, but equally significant is the strange phenomenon of Billy's death. There is a suggestion that Billy ironically cheats the gallows by dying a providential death moments before the execution. The religious symbolism surrounding the hanging suggests a divine tableau in which nature intervenes and protests the injustice of Billy's death by allowing him a providential and painless death before being hanged. The Lamb of God symbolizes not only the sacrificial victim but also liberation from pain and death. To view the story as ironic in intent is thus to misconstrue it when viewed in context. On the other hand, to say that Billy achieves salvation is not to arrive at a transcendental point beyond optimism and pessimism, beyond belief and doubt. If he intends us to feel that Billy has gone to heaven, then Melville is simply a believer and nothing more complex can be construed from this. It is hard to accept the argument that Billy does achieve salvation. He was not religious, and Melville furthermore refers to the chaplain as "incongruous" on a man-of-war. Though Billy does cheat the gallows, it is hardly clear that his death is "providential."

William Braswell
MELVILLE'S BILLY BUDD AS "AN INSIDE NARRATIVE"
AL, XXIX (May 1957), 133-146

Billy Budd symbolizes Melville's own heart in mutiny against his head; this is the "Inside Narrative." Billy is the heart and Claggart the head, able (like Vere) in this depraved world to understand—but never to be—the innocent, Christlike heart. Young Melville maintained a healthy balance between them: heart strolled gaily above-deck while head schemed below. Then rebellion arose, from *Mardi* through *Moby-Dick*, climaxed by Billy's blow to the head. Melville sympathized with the heart's Christian idealism, but recognized its folly. When the good heart (Ahab, Billy) struck at evil (whale, Claggart), it also blasphemed and mutinied against agents of divine authority; when Pierre, all heart, fought evil with ideal love, insanity and hatred followed. Accepting Plinlimmon's counsel, Melville found Christ's wisdom unsuited to earth. The heart's rebellion had run wild and threatened to destroy state, ship, and self. Vere's ship, during wartime, is threatened by mutiny—just as Melville, overwrought after writing *Pierre,* was threatened by insanity—and Vere (Latin *vir: man*) portrays how he quelled the mutiny of his youthful heart (*baby* Budd). Mature Melville-Vere prefers nature and love but, with his superior intellect, is a realist and dutifully chooses king and necessity. The enemy's threat is imminent. Mutiny, defeat, and anarchy will destroy man unless the head upholds the King's law and destroys the rebellious heart. Proving the head's virtue, the disciplined *Indomitable* vanquishes the enemy. And Vere gives his own life for forms, sanity, and social order. Even more than Billy, Vere suffers in his choice, but this is the cross man must bear when, like Abraham, he is willing to sacrifice Isaac in obedience to the only principles that work in this man-of-war world.

John B. Noone, Jr.
BILLY BUDD: TWO CONCEPTS OF NATURE
AL, XXIX (November 1957), 249-262

In *Billy Budd,* Melville seeks an ideal suited to actual men and finds it in history, not in utopian theories. No single panacea suits the world's complexity. Billy exemplifies Rousseau's noble savage, able through instinct alone to flourish in a pure state of nature (aboard *The Rights of*

Man). But he is morally immature, innocent not by choice but by ignorance of good and evil, and unattuned to this world. Paradoxically, what guarantees his freedom is his enemy, Hobbes' *Leviathan*. Claggart exemplifies Hobbes' depraved primitive, able only through rational rules to impose peace in a savage world, for total war characterizes man's natural, instinctive state. Peace, the highest good of which man is capable, is gained through war against bestial instinct; only reason, working through abstract forms, ruthless discipline, and technology—the seventy-four-gun *Indomitable*—guarantees peace. But if Billy or Claggart were given command, either one would destroy the ship, since in this world, neither concept of nature—innocence or depravity—offers a possible ideal. The next possibility is detachment; Vere, seeking ultimate laws and forms, exemplifies Newton's mechanical reason. Yet Vere's reason, not Billy, is on trial; his irrelevant arguments trap the intellectually innocent court with reason, and Vere is insane for equating his sterile, rationally ordered world with that of living men. Only Lord Nelson meets the test of experience. He knows the limits of mechanical forms, chooses to reject them, dares to inspire (not subjugate) his men with his own, personal nobility of character, and leads them to victory. His synthesis of reason and instinct offers man, in his less than utopian society, a possible ideal.

Richard Harter Fogle

BILLY BUDD: ACCEPTANCE OR IRONY

TSE, VIII (1958), 107–113

Although *Billy Budd* is ironic, it is not ironic in the sense of meaning something other than it seems to say, but neither does it contain painful mockery. It is ironic in the modern sense of the term: it means something more than it seems to say. The story is, in addition, a nineteenth-century Aristotelian tragedy. The characters are exceptional men, elevated by associations with heroic legend, history and myth, and in the story there is a tragic discrepancy between the real and the ideal. Claggart's murder is divine justice, but aboard the *Indomitable*, Billy must be tried under wartime conditions for the murder of his superior officer. The law of the mutiny act must judge this "angel of God," and the unfallen Billy must be found guilty by the law of a fallen world. The real world and the ideal world can never fuse. This is further demonstrated by the mutiny at the Nore and the Revolution, which are also types of a second Fall of Man.

Billy Budd further meets the requirements of classical tragedy in that the characters suffer *peripateia*, or ironic reversal: Vere's well-laid plans result in the death of Claggart and the execution of Billy. Reconciliation, yet another element of classical tragedy which is presented in Billy's death, brings about a kind of partial redemption, for his defeat and passion are able to provide some kind of hope for the future as his story lives on after his death. The element of tragedy that is the irony of fate is also contained in *Billy Budd*, but Melville's irony is not of a diminishing, wailing or mocking nature; it is deepening, enriching, and intensifying.

Phil Withim

BILLY BUDD: TESTAMENT OF RESISTANCE

MLQ, XX (June 1959), 115-127

Billy Budd is no testament of acceptance. To think that Melville *reconciles* instinctive good (Billy) with civilized evil (Claggart) is to misinterpret Vere's crucial role. Vere is a Claggart—a perverted intellect. Ironically, he reads widely only to reinforce his narrow views (serving king, not nature). Likewise, he uses the court to sanction (not guide) his judgment against Billy. He claims concern for his men's welfare, but considers them beasts to be controlled by forms, discipline, reason. Yet he uses fear, not reason, to persuade his officers. Corrupting reason, he rationalizes that man must submit to unjust laws, accept necessity, and enforce tyranny. In short, he is insanely expedient and perpetrates the basest sin—prudence. In ironic contrast, Lord Nelson disdained prudence and inspired mutineers with loyalty; he served the King best with persuasion, not coercion. With greater irony, Billy dies blessing Vere; he transcends forms by trusting in Vere, who rules with forms because he trusts no man; like Nelson and unlike Vere, Billy (Christ, Isaac) dies nobly. It remains for living men to be noble, too. Melville dedicates *Billy Budd* to Jack Chase, who fought for human rights; he prefaces it with praise for the French Revolution; he admonishes men's leaders to resist institutionalized forms, for while men may be flawed, they are not beasts to be chained. He advocates revolution. If it succeeds, man can be free from hereditary tyranny, but if it fails, man becomes a Billy Budd suffering tyranny's abuses because, innocent and trusting, he fails to resist. Then heaven is man's only hope. But Melville never fully accepts heaven as panacea and, with scathing irony, he continues the fight on earth.

Warner Berthoff
"CERTAIN PHENOMENAL MEN": THE EXAMPLE OF BILLY BUDD
ELH, XXVII (1960), 334-351

Billy Budd is not so much concerned with an allegorical definition of universal truth as it is an attempt to "define and denominate certain phenomenal men." Rather than asking, "What is life?" or "What are the workings of God?," Billy Budd asks, "Given certain circumstances, what kind of response is there in certain phenomenal men?" The theme thus concerns the actions of magnanimity under the most tormenting worldly constraint. Billy, Vere, and Claggart are each depicted as some kind of natural force with their actions proceeding from their capacity of spirit. Claggart manifests iniquity. Vere and Billy manifest magnanimity, a particular greatness of soul, touched with divinity, which elevates and unites them in a mutual "sacrament." Melville's intent is to show Vere and Billy joined together in a complementary magnanimity, a natural greatness of soul like that admired by Milton. Thus *Billy Budd* depicts a kind of apotheosis of human nature. On the one side is horrible depravity, on the other are two kinds of magnanimity self-realized through acknowledgment of each other. Baudelaire has written, "The only great ones among mankind are the poet, the priest, and the soldier; the man who sings, the man who blesses, and the man who sacrifices, and sacrifices himself." Vere is the soldier-priest joined in magnanimity with Billy, who has the power to bless and transfigure his life and the lives of others. Melville, the artist, is the "singer" with magnanimity.

C. B. Ives

BILLY BUDD AND THE ARTICLES OF WAR
AL, XXXIV (March 1962), 31-39

Captain Vere, difficult to allegorize (as Divine Justice or Tyranny), is a realistic and human character. The Articles of War were his excuse for hanging Billy, his deep-seated motives the cause. Despite Vere's claim that Billy's case was dire (Melville did make it severe, altering the actual *Somers* trial), hanging was not his only option. Vere invoked the Mutiny Act, which was not applicable to sailors, and the Articles of War, which for persons convicted of striking officers required the death sentence by a general court-martial—not by Vere's summary court-martial. Yet Vere knew that, by custom, captains had wide powers to be harsh (hanging mutineers and murderers, though he saw Billy as neither) or lenient, un-bound by the Articles of War. His options were to pardon, lightly punish, or hang Billy, or to wait for a general court-martial. The hanging, with Vere's urgency, secrecy, and obsession with the form rather than the spirit of judicial inquiry, grievously surprised his officers. His trial arguments, directed against nature, human sympathy, and conscience, revealed a personal conflict. Vere's quest for factual truth resulted in habitual self-punishment and denial; he became a humorless bachelor, turning from his vital sea life to dry, bookish facts and rejection of all feminine sympathies. But he could neither hide nor quite destroy his emotions. Billy suddenly roused his heart. In Vere's *inside-narrative* conflict (heart vs. ascetic discipline), Billy had struck Claggart. Using the Articles of War to mask his insanity, Vere, like Abraham, struck back and sacrificed Billy, a stern, heart-denying passion again commanding his will.

Charles A. Reich

THE TRAGEDY OF JUSTICE IN BILLY BUDD

YR, LVI (Spring 1967), 368-389

Rational, materialistic society fails to accept, as Melville finally did, the mixture of good and evil which is man's nature and which gives life its fullness. In *Billy Budd*, Melville examines this theme in terms of a three-part problem in law. *Legal Standards.* Representing natural forces, Billy and Claggart must inevitably clash; thus Billy kills through necessity, not free choice, and under natural law is innocent. Yet natural law neither supports order nor checks chaos; if society is to be protected from savage nature, then man's law must reject necessity, must assume free choice (the exercise of free will), and must therefore judge appearances—the objective act rather than man's nature. *Vere's Reactions.* Faced with the conflict between natural and social law, Vere has no choice. He would prefer to spare Billy but feels compelled to quell latent mutiny, and the Mutiny Act allows no exceptions. But his reactions are in no way rigid. Vere is unusually sensitive; from holding pat convictions, he grows into an agonized awareness that, in executing the law which duty dictates, he must sacrifice values higher than man's laws. His suffering leads to the third problem. *Society's Standards.* The execution scene focuses on society's rejection of human nature, its blindness to the fact that both nature and man are flawed. Society's law mistakes the flaws (acts) for the whole man

and, to protect man against savage acts, destroys him. But those who witness Billy's hanging still recognize and feel his humanity and thereby reveal the gulf between their spiritual knowledge and their practices. They feel compassion and know his innocence yet blindly act according to artificial, utilitarian standards and narrow extremes of right and wrong. This two-valued orientation alienates social man from natural man. Lest we forget, Melville reminds us that there is more to man than laws or reasoned forms allow. By such reminder and by opening our eyes to our self-made prisons, Melville fulfills the artist's role in modern society.

Alice Chandler
THE NAME SYMBOLISM OF CAPTAIN VERE
NCF, XXI (June 1967), 86-89

Critics of *Billy Budd* have generally claimed that Melville chose the name Vere to suggest either truth (*veritas*) or manliness (*vir*). However, the character of Captain Vere lends itself to no such simplistic explanation, and the name Vere may have other connotations. Although Vere, as the family name of the Earls of Oxford, did suggest chivalry in the nineteenth century, the name was often used pejoratively. Novels by Scott, Lever, and Hood all use the name Vere unfavorably, as does Tennyson's familiar poem, "Lady Clara Vere de Vere," which tells how a high-born dame drove her lowly lover to suicide. Thus Melville may have unconsciously chosen the name for its popular connotations of snobbishness and cruelty rather than those of nobility and honor. Such a reading would support the "democratic" interpretation of *Billy Budd.* *

Ralph W. Willett
NELSON AND VERE: HERO AND VICTIM IN BILLY BUDD, SAILOR
PMLA, LXXXII (October 1967), 370-376

Whereas the historical personage of Lord Nelson in *Billy Budd, Sailor* represents for Melville the "ideal version of the governing principle," the fictional figure of Vere is limited morally and professionally by his own temperament and by the circumstances in which he finds himself. However, Melville tempers his criticism of Vere with sympathy; he recognizes the captain's difficulties in an unpredictable, ironic universe.

Parallels are perceived between Melville's conception of Nelson and the theories of Carlyle in *Lectures on Hero-Worship and the Heroic in History*. Melville's Nelson corresponds to Carlyle's "hero as king," that is, the hero as a stabilizing figure, psychologically equipped to control insurrections; unlike Vere, he can neutralize chance by the mere force of his personality. The stages of development in the novella are traced in order to show how Melville proceeded to emphasize the essential contrast between Nelson and Vere; Melville's various revisions of his text are also examined at length for the same purpose. A consideration of Melville's earlier treatment of Nelson in *White-Jacket* initiates a survey of Melville's attitude towards naval figures and towards discipline and order. Nelson's qualities are discovered in Jack Chase, and the inadequacies of Vere are detected in Amasa Delano. Finally it is suggested that the social and political climate of the post Civil War period intensified Melville's dread of public conflict, and induced in him a nostalgia for the past and its socially cohesive hero types, such as Nelson.*

Roland A. Duerksen

THE DEEP QUANDARY IN <u>BILLY BUDD</u>

NEQ, XLI (March 1968), 51-66

Melville's *Billy Budd* is neither a call to violent rebellion nor a declaration of preference for established law over individual choice. Instead, it essentially embodies a basic question about a power system that has almost universal acceptance despite its diametric opposition to society's highest moral values. All the major characters acquiesce in this power system. Captain Vere, a torn man, overcomes the intellectual side of his character to align himself ponderously with the status quo—thus finding the basic responsibility for Billy's death to be not really his, but the Navy's or War's. The inverse—that society uses Vere's specific responsibility to shield itself from conscious guilt—seems equally clear. By his unquestioning acceptance of impressment into service on a ship of war, Billy agrees to being deprived of a world in which his natural, primitive, untainted humanity has been able to thrive. This acquiescence in his own depersonalization leads finally to his pronouncing a blessing upon Vere, his judge and executioner. John Claggart, a sinister and unnatural man who has risen rapidly in the power system, is threatened by Billy's essential humanity and instigates his destruction in the machine of violence which has conquered Vere's intellectuality. In an effective characterization of the Chaplain, a comparatively minor figure, Melville clearly depicts the institutionalization of violence—its espousal even by the religion of the Prince of Peace. Yet Billy himself most emphatically exposes the ironic situation of a society which cannot put into practice its highest ideals. It is a philosophic problem that Melville apparently was unable to solve.*

THE CONFIDENCE-MAN

(1857)

Richard Chase
MELVILLE'S CONFIDENCE-MAN
KR, XI (Winter 1949), 122-140

The Confidence-Man (1857) is a subtle, buoyant satire of the American temperament, as well as a folklore book. The *Fidèle* is a microcosm of life in the United States on which the passengers form an American tableau. The Confidence-Man dons a variety of masks, partly based upon such folklore figures as the Yankee Peddler, the Westerner, the Uncouth Rustic, Orpheus-Prometheus, Uncle Sam, and at one point, Christ. The final episode symbolizes the attempt of the youthful Prometheus to warn the Old God that he must face life's threatening challenges. He tries to awaken the sleeping inhabitants of the planet. The Confidence-Man, however, tries to convince the Old God that all is right with the universe. In short, the book is an attack by a liberal upon liberalism, for the Confidence-Man exhibits all the evils of liberalism in Melville's time. He is superficial, fond of morally elevating rhetoric, materialistic, spuriously optimistic, wishfully vague, facile in his blind faith in progress. The job of the Confidence-Man is to cloud moral distinctions and prevent men from making choices. Neutrality is desired by liberals in times of crisis, and the Confidence-Man's white suit signifies neutrality. Melville is suggesting the universe can no longer recognize moral distinctions. The liberal, deficient in self-knowledge and fooled by himself into thinking he is innocuous, is denounced by Melville for his irresponsibility and lack of self-awareness about the consequences of moral choices. Devoted to destroying the myth of the Fall of Man, *The Confidence-Man* constitutes Melville's criticism of liberalism.

John G. Cawelti
SOME NOTES ON THE STRUCTURE OF THE CONFIDENCE-MAN
AL, XXIX (November 1957), 278-288

Though condemned as a philosophical potpourri, digressive and disunified, *The Confidence-Man* is structured to reflect Melville's perception of reality. Beneath the shimmering surface masks of nature and man lie fathomless depths, inscrutable and ambiguous—the cosmic enigmas and man's ever-shifting motivations. Yet, like Moby-Dick rising, reality sometimes breaks through the mask; Melville's art portrays these fleeting, start-ling glimpses. Three philosophical digressions reveal the novel's frame (ambiguity) and key (reversal). In the first (Chapter 16), a dense, inane country merchant suddenly glimpses reality and speaks with momentary brilliance, but this insight passes, may only have been a delusion, and leads to nothing but ambiguity. Throughout the novel, such reversals present a clue, then destroy it with a contrary clue too weak to support a new interpretation. These antitheses (e.g., pursuer-pursued, lies-truths, comedy-tragedy) form a maze of contradictory, unresolved clues, and thus the novel's meaning remains ambiguous. Similarly, the second digression (Chapter 33) argues both for realism and romanticism in art. In the third (Chapter 44), the cosmopolitan Confidence-Man exemplifies reality; he is many-faced man and the many-masked cosmos man faces, his destiny unknowable; artistically and philosophically, he is a revolving beacon lighting every action, object, and person around him, and a vortex pulling everything back to his focus and genesis. Thus the novel's artistic structure mirrors and portrays reality as Melville sees it; it juggles appearances with realities, leads man through kaleidoscoping masks into mazes, and leaves him there to face enigma alone. No bitter, philosophical put-on, *The Confidence-Man* is Melville's deliberate and ingenious representation of cosmic ambiguity.

Edward H. Rosenberry

MELVILLE'S SHIP OF FOOLS

PMLA, LXXV (December 1960), 604-608

In *The Confidence-Man: His Masquerade,* Melville once again probes moral evil in a ship microcosm. He had previously allegorized vicious humanity in *White-Jacket's* man-of-war, with devil Bland masked as a gentleman. *The Confidence-Man* develops Bland's morality type; it pulls all characters together into a sinister, ambiguous, organic evil; beating time to *fool fool fool,* it takes place on All Fools' Day. Its prototype is Brant's fifteenth-century German anatomy of folly, *The Ship of Fools,* exceed-ingly popular throughout sixteenth-century Europe. Perhaps Melville read it (his Belial-like portrait of the Confidence-Man resembles Brant's study of unrighteousness), or perhaps he knew of its tradition through such Jacobean writers as Burton and Jonson. Burton's *Anatomy of Melancholy* foreshadows both Melville's narrative structure and his theme of moral masquerade, that "Life is a pic-nic *en costume,*" for roles merge ambigu-ously as victim and victimizer wear the same costume (folly type). Melville is known to have read Ben Jonson, a master of masque and satire; in tone, *The Confidence-Man* resembles Jonson's *Volpone*, and in material and treatment, *Bartholomew Fair.* The anonymous *Cock Lorell's Boat* is in the same tradition; Melville may have known it directly or through Jonson's *The Gypsies Metamorphosed*, a masquerade in which Cock Lorell serves human sinners to the devil at a banquet, much like Melville's menu, epicurian devil, and costumed picnic. Whether or not Melville read or used these sources, clearly *The Confidence-Man* is in *The Ship of Fools* tradition where satire's whip lashes at optimism and unmasks moral hypocrisy.

Walter Dubler
THEME AND STRUCTURE IN MELVILLE'S THE CONFIDENCE-MAN
AL, XXXIII (November 1961), 307-319

Melville chastizes evil American attitudes in *The Confidence-Man,* yet is no nihilist for omitting positive alternatives; his satire implies a norm, some possibility of hope. His simple vehicle is the riverboat microcosm, a cross section of America in the Mississippi mainstream, but complex dramatic techniques develop his theme. The major dramatic form is a dialectical pattern of thesis-antithesis, but without a stated synthesis (or satiric norm). Thus, while the pattern portrays extremism as evil in increasingly somber episodes, it is constantly counterpointed by the unstated, implied norm—the Golden Mean. The pattern begins with extremes of charity (white and black confidence-men, too distrustful and trusting, are both evil) and continues with extremes of faith and optimism: an inventor and herb-doctor call science and then nature the absolute panacea; transcendental optimists naively theorize about man's beautiful nature but in practice mistrust it. At the novel's heart, Moredock, with his extreme pessimism, is an Indian-hating monomaniac. Thus what could be virtues in moderation become, in excess, evils, and the implication is that as long as America condones extremism, it will be blind to the complex, inscrutable realities of nature and man, unable to achieve a healthy, workable balance. The dramatic pattern shows that theories unattuned to practice are shams and only hide cruel practices under benevolent masks; at the end, Bible-reading Old America calls businessman New America a public benefactor, though he is a hustler in practice. With modern American society masquerading as benevolent while intent on fraud, the future looks dim. Melville warns that this ongoing masquerade will consume the flame of hope, truth, and moderation.

Leon F. Seltzer
CAMUS'S ABSURD AND THE WORLD OF MELVILLE'S CONFIDENCE-MAN
PMLA, LXXXII (March 1967), 14-27

Melville's moral and metaphysical position in *The Confidence-Man* reveals itself through the novel's overall design. The book bears several important affinities to Albert Camus's notions of the absurd, as they are elucidated in that writer's extended philosophical essay, *The Myth of Sisyphus.* References to selected descriptions of the absurd creator, the absurd creation, and the absurd man in *The Myth,* demonstrate how these characterizations may profitably be related to Melville's novel. In *The Confidence-Man,* Melville, by focusing his lens on a master swindler, systematically demonstrates the feeble grounds for belief and may thus be viewed as an absurd creator. In addition, his unorthodox hero—the uncommonly intellectual trickster—may be understood as the epitome of the absurd man. Conceived as a nihilist of tremendous lucidity, he implies through his every act a profound awareness and rejection of man's almost irrepressible urge to negate or "transcend" his reason in order to satisfy his gnawing hunger for faith. The very structure of the book, in its methodical perversion of the three classical unities, is calculated to betray the essential chaos of the universe and thereby expose the baselessness of confidence. The world of *The Confidence-Man,* where the position of trust remains wholly unrelated to human situations, clearly invalidates the Pauline gospel of charity, which the author perceived as man's only hope. Consequently, though the novel can be interpreted morally as speaking in behalf of Christian, or selfless, love, its ultimate meaning is that such an ethic of charity is sadly untenable.*

Edward Mitchell
FROM ACTION TO ESSENCE: SOME NOTES ON THE STRUCTURE OF MELVILLE'S THE CONFIDENCE-MAN
AL, XL (March 1968), 27-37

The majority of Melville's critics tend to take one of two views regarding the structure of *The Confidence-Man.* The first sees the structure as merely ostensible. The argument runs that the novel is essentially dialectical, but that it lacks the embodied precept or fixed point, either of character or theme, which would permit a comprehensible resolution. The other basic approach argues that the novel is essentially an allegory, albeit a multileveled one, and that it is properly read largely in the same manner as any other allegory. The most striking feature of *The Confidence-Man* is not embodied in precepts but rather in repetitive activity manifest in the numerous confrontations between confidence-man and victim. Within this novel there are only two basic characters—confidence-men and victims— but the two are only distinguishable in terms of their function. Thus any man who puts confidence in another is a potential, if not actual, victim, just as any man who solicits confidence from another is a potential, if not actual, confidence-man. Moreover, there are no confrontations in the novel which do not entail either a direct solicitation for confidence in something in particular, or have as the topic of discussion the subject of confidence itself, which in turn requires the individuals involved to place either confidence in confidence, or confidence in something else. Thus the further implication is that this entire "Anacharsis Cloots congress of all kinds of that multiform pilgrim species, man" is itself distinguishable in terms of the one, single, continuous activity which is the *sine qua non* of its existence, which in turn suggests that any individual who can neither solicit nor place confidence is outside the realm of humanity.*

Joseph Baim
THE CONFIDENCE-MAN AS "TRICKSTER"
ATQ, No. 1 (I Quarter 1969), 81-83

An important clue to the character of the Confidence-Man may well be revealed if we view him as a "trickster," a figure which I understand to be archetypal, in the Jungian sense of the term: the personification of a primordial image out of the collective unconscious. The trickster's outstanding characteristic is that he functions ambivalently, and like Melville's con-man, his origins are obscure; he is faceless, at times perfectly known, at times mysterious, a kind of "punster," who has things both ways. Like Hermes, the prototypal Greek trickster, Melville's con-man is a crosser of boundaries, a "transfer agent" who breaks out of the confines of the habitual self, accepts both the benign and the bestial face of human experience and, in so doing, points the way to fulfillment. The Confidence-Man is ascendent because he is in touch with both God and the Devil; he succeeds in rising above the consistency sanctioned by conventional, societal values. He represents, in fine, Melville's notion that the life-spirit is contained in a *tertium quid*—in the tension between perfectly figured contraries.*

PIERRE

(1852)

Tyrus Hillway
PIERRE, THE FOOL OF VIRTUE
AL, XXI (May 1949), 201-211

Scholars are mistaken who find Melville's philosophy neatly defined in *Pierre's* Plinlimmon pamphlet—which advocates (since Christ prescribed heavenly rather than earthly conduct) heeding man's animal rather than spiritual dictates. Melville is no philosopher; he presents rather than solves moral problems. Taji, Ahab, and Pierre search vainly for truth. Pierre begins by choosing Christ-like, disinterested virtue over earthly expediency; he heeds what he considers God's counsel and, if betrayed, promises fierce defiance. Then he suffers and doubts. Nothing offers help but his own idealistic counsel, all else being absurdity and ambiguity. Plinlimmon (and Emerson) vainly claim answers, and Father Mapple counterpoints Plinlimmon in *Moby-Dick* in the belief that to obey God is to disobey self, which is hard. But God is silent. And it is difficult even to know self; flawed with self-satisfied pride, virtuous Pierre is blind to evil. The deeper he thinks, the more he realizes his impure passions, the insincerity of man's ideals, the elusiveness of truth. He finds himself not free but fated, manipulated by a not clearly benevolent puppetmaster. His philosophical quest ends in frustrating limitation, with earth and soul unreconciled. Disillusioned and despairing of certainty, Pierre strikes like Ahab against the only tangible evil he can find, his cousin—a final, defiant gesture against absurdity. Thus Melville, though hinting that self-knowledge may set man free, is one of our earliest determinists. Only the mature Billy Budd finds Christ-like heroism in his martyrdom. Meanwhile, defiant Pierre finds himself the fool of Truth, Virtue, and Fate.

William Braswell
THE EARLY LOVE SCENES IN MELVILLE'S PIERRE
AL, XXII (1950), 283-289

It may be hard to know Melville's intent in *Pierre,* but its purple prose is not as trashy as many critics suggest. Indeed, Melville's style in the early love scenes is mock romantic, satirizing the conventions of the sentimental, erotic romances. He ridicules Pierre's precious posturing, setting it off with grave, Hebraic cadences. He satirizes idyllic Eden, setting it up for contrast with the final prison scene. Typically, Melville loved exaggeration. In the early love scenes, extravagant characterization breeds extravagant dialogue, matching the idealistic, sentimental setting. In his ludicrous paeans on earth's beauty he even outdoes the giftbooks of his day. In all, it is with irony and farfetched conceits that he mocks the gospel of love and the religion of the heart. Perhaps in this mannerism Melville is laughing derisively at his own early, spiritual innocence, just as he elevates Pierre's extravagant felicity before his fall into violence, hatred, and degradation. Melville was not, as his critics charge, confused and insecure in his intention or bound by stylistic consistency. He gave rein to wild humor when it suited. Surely his purpose in the love scene was clear when he described sailors tying love knots; he knew their uncouthness well.

Charles Moorman

MELVILLE'S <u>PIERRE</u> AND THE FORTUNATE FALL

AL, XXV (March 1953), 13-30

No mere allegory, *Pierre* is particular in its conventional (but shoddy) tale and universal in its symbolic imagery which, in the first half of the book, develops a theme vital to Melville's philosophy—the Fortunate Fall. Idyllic Eden preludes the Fall. Innocent Pierre, replacing his dead father, is to be lord of this feudal aristocracy and is imaged as shepherd-king, courtly lover, and Christian knight-errant dreaming of a sister to love and save. Like green, golden Paradise, angelic Lucy is described in bright, idealized images of sight. Pierre takes this American Eden at face value, but Melville undermines appearances with images of vulgar, democratic realities. Pastoral, courtly, and aristocratic Christian traditions are seen as irrelevant and Paradise as a delusion. Idyllic images become ambiguous as Isabel strips away Pierre's veil, revealing his self-made idols to be false guides, and hard, cold, dark, serpentine images of the Fall ensue: the pine (Tree of Life, Isabel, fertility, violence, sea) is opposed to the hemlock (Tree of Death, Lucy, sterility, comfort, land). Isabel initiates the Quest myth. Pierre dies to be reborn, follows the call to encounter disillusionment and defeat, to know his Father, and to return with divine grace to aid mankind. The Fall is fortunate in that, like Job, Pierre gains knowledge of both good and evil, unknown in Eden. Isabel, with Fall and Quest images, leads him to this knowledge. Thus Melville establishes a pattern leading the hero to victorious transfiguration and sets the stage for tragic frustration in the last half of *Pierre.*

James Kissane
IMAGERY, MYTH, AND MELVILLE'S PIERRE

AL, XXVI (January 1955), 564-572

Charles Moorman ("Melville's *Pierre* and the Fortunate Fall") tried to define the novel's structure through archetypal imagery alone and thus found a Fortunate Fall dichotomy between idyllic Paradise illusion and vulgar American reality, and between Lucy (sterility, hemlock, Tree of Death) and Isabel (fertility, pine, Tree of Life). But imagery alone, especially when warped to fit a myth, is a limited approach to pattern and meaning. Though Fall images occur, other images represent Lucy as vital and Isabel as deadly. Melville portrays ambiguity—not a good-evil, illusion-disillusion dichotomy but an identity. Pierre's dilemma is that he must reconcile opposite images of one absolute. The myth explains neither the first half of *Pierre* nor the last (where victorious transfiguration and return do not apply). Typically, the approach to fiction through archetypal patterns is rigid. It may be valid with static, plotless novels which emphasize one attitude and where analysis of one part may define the whole, but it fails with dynamic novels which emphasize process and where meaning comes through relationships in a plot sequence. The meaning of *Pierre* is defined in terms of dramatic, not archetypal, pattern: Pierre moves through disillusionment toward ambiguity, toward awareness that good and evil are not only reflections of the same truth but are meaningless and that moral virtue is irrelevant. The Fortunate Fall approach is equally irrelevant. Myth-minded Moorman clutched *Pierre*'s tail and thought Melville's elephant an archetypal snake.

Nathalia Wright
PIERRE: HERMAN MELVILLE'S INFERNO

AL, XXXII (May 1960), 167-181

Pierre is Melville's anatomy of sin, a hell journey closely paralleling Dante's in narrative detail, sequence, and theme. The first half parallels Dante's Cantos 1-8. In Saddle Meadows (no paradise), all suffer the sins of Incontinence: his parents are carnal and proud, Pierre himself is gluttonous (compensating for sexual immaturity) and wrathful in his frustrating search for truth. Imagery links him with fiends, sin, and the dark descent. The second half of *Pierre* parallels Dante's City of Dis and the last four

Circles of Hell. As Pierre enters the city (with its river and Charon and chaotic din), Malebolge is the setting; he meets Dantean sinners and is one himself, guilty of Violence (against neighbors, God, Nature, Art) and the sins of Simple Fraud. Titanlike, he rebels against God and, in winter cold, exhibits hellpit's Compound Frauds (betraying kin, country, guests, bene-factors). Finally he writes a blasphemous, hypocritical, world-hating book. Like Dante, Pierre sees society rampant with Fraud, but unlike Dante's traveller, Pierre is immature. He lacks Virgil, divine reason's guidance. He lacks Lucia, Dante's spiritual salvation through sex; though Pierre calls Lucy and Isabel angels of love, he cannot rise above incontinent appetite. Following heart-feeling alone, Pierre himself is a fiend and suffers hell. He is without perspective, and unaware of purgatory and paradise, hopelessly hellbound. He writes not from experience but from books and is as mean-ingless a fragment of life as his book. And thus, for writers who try to reconcile this world's Fraud with moral ideals there is a clear similarity with Pierre; they are themselves frauds.

Rita Gollin

PIERRE'S METAMORPHOSIS OF DANTE'S <u>INFERNO</u>

AL, XXXIX, (January 1968), 542-545

Melville modified his borrowings from Dante's *Inferno* especially in two scenes of *Pierre*. Pierre's dream of Enceladus in detail and sequence recalls Dante's giants of Canto XXXI. Enceladus, armless antagonist of divine power, resembles Dante's Ephialtes; but Dante learns the futility of rebellion, while Pierre identifies with the suffering rebel. The prison where Pierre is confined after murdering his cousin recalls the cold weight-bearing pit of hell containing traitors to kin whose tears freeze. Melville uses Dante's details but identifies scene and sinner: Pierre himself seems to bear the weight above him, and the dungeon seems to weep. Although Dante emerges to see starlight, Pierre dies in darkness, in a "gulf of guilt" which proves incomprehensible and insurmountable. The ultimate mordant ambiguity of *Pierre* is that Pierre's idealistic quest ends with Pierre himself the impenitent chief sinner and central cause of suffering, like the arch-rebel Satan. This metamorphosis is Melville's major inversion of Dante's vision, intensifying the book's anguished pessimism.*

R. L. Carothers

MELVILLE'S "CENCI": A PORTRAIT OF <u>PIERRE</u>

BSUF, X (Winter 1969), 53-59

An identification of the nature of the father-son relationships in *Pierre* is essential to an understanding of that novel. Pierre's attitude towards his mother is incestuous, and in order to avoid conflict with the image of his dead father, Pierre hides his more basic urges behind a facade of compensatory idealism. When he discovers that he has an illegitimate sister, however, that facade is forever cracked, and Pierre begins an assault on the father through an attempt to have another of the "old man's women." His heretofore unshakable faith in himself is soon shattered, too, as he discovers that not only is the father an ambiguous figure, but that the son too cannot be known even by himself. The accomplishment of this insight is gradual, but it is complete when Pierre sees an objectification of himself in the portrait by Guido of Beatrice Cenci which he discovers hanging in a French gallery, enigmatically facing a painting of a man who is the image of Pierre's father. Father and son thus symbolically meet at last and their meeting leads quickly to the final destruction of the son.*

MARDI

(1849)

Gordon H. Mills
THE SIGNIFICANCE OF "ARCTURUS" IN MARDI
AL, XIV (1942), 158-161

The blood-red star, Arcturus, is Melville's central symbol in *Mardi.* Once we see this, we can no longer doubt the novel's unity. *Mardi* opens with the whaling ship, *Arcturion,* and closes with the red star dominant, as the protagonist Taji continues his pursuit of Yillah. Of the several references throughout the book, one especially links Taji with Arcturus—the sons of the priest he murdered pursue him over the sea, guided by the star. Though many mythological references to Arcturus were available to Melville, he used none of them. The key to his symbolism is found in a magazine called *Arcturus* (1840-42). It was published by good friends of his, the Duyckinck brothers, whose private library he used before writing *Mardi* (1849). The key reference comes from the prologue to the first issue of the magazine, in which it is proposed that Arcturus and its inhabitants look keenly down upon men's follies and errors. This view is not only paralleled by nearly identical passages in *Mardi* but represents Melville's very theme—that to view man correctly we must adopt an impartial viewpoint. Thus Yillah and Arcturus (Taji) are complementary symbols: Yillah symbolizes the positive goal of happiness and peace and Arcturus the negative, independent viewpoint of detached criticism. This symbolism of Arcturus not only reveals *Mardi*'s central theme but suggests the direction of thought in Melville's later works.

Merrell R. Davis
THE FLOWER SYMBOLISM IN MARDI
MLQ, II (1942), 625-638

In 1841 Mrs. Frances Osgood edited *The Poetry of Flowers and Flowers of Poetry,* including a "Copious Floral Dictionary." Typical of the "flower books" so popular between 1825 and 1865, it is helpful in examining the flower symbolism of Melville's *Mardi.* In almost all cases, the symbolic meanings attached to the various flowers in Mrs. Osgood's "dictionary" closely parallel the interpretations given by Yoomy to the flower messages of Hautia, and occasionally the two are identically phrased. Mrs. Osgood's book is thus both a representative of the "flower books" of the era and a valid source for interpreting the flower symbolism in *Mardi.* The descriptive imagery in the novel suggests Yillah's identification with the lily; the characteristics of the "Valley of Ardair" closely resemble the descriptions of the habitat of the lily of the valley in Mrs. Osgood's book. Hautia is clearly identified as a flower, and flower symbolism is seen in Taji's quest for Yillah, signifying a quest for the Return of Happiness. In addition to her flower messages, Hautia gifts Taji with flowers which symbolize Witchcraft, Desire, Sensibility, Intoxication, and Charity. Her other gifts symbolize Crushed Hopes, Death, the Crushed Return of Happiness, and Deceitful Hopes. Hautia's desire for Taji and her opposition to Yillah are symbolized by her flower messages. Queen Hautia is a "dahlia on its stalk," or Heartless Beauty. She bears an amaryllis, or Haughtiness. (Her name may be a play on *haughty.*) She wears a vervain girdle (Enchantment) and crushes pinks (Lively and Pure Affection) and lilies (Purity and Modesty). But the "scentless" Queen disappoints Taji, and he pursues his quest for Yillah, who, identified with the lily of the valley, represents the Return of Happiness. Thus Mrs. Osgood's "floral dictionary" affords a credible interpretation of Yillah and Hautia and suggests that Taji is on a quest for the Return of Happiness, though he succumbs to the Heartless Beauty. In Mrs. Osgood's "dial of flowers" there is the moral lesson of the futility of man's quest for happiness.

Tyrus Hillway

TAJI'S QUEST FOR CERTAINTY

AL, XVIII (March 1946), 27-34

The fifth pilgrim in *Mardi* prefigures Taji's quest and the central allegory, that man is meant to live on the plain, not the peak. The pilgrim seeks to climb Mt. Ofo, the way to Truth. He refuses to be guided there by blind Pani, who admires his courage but recognizes that knowledge is doubt disguised as religion. He will be guided to Truth only by his own, God-given reason, yet with this noble instinct he opposes doctrinal rites and Oro's priests sacrifice him. Similarly, Taji seeks Yillah, Ultimate Truth. With his noble instinct he saves Yillah from institutionalized superstition by killing the priest who would sacrifice her, yet the priest's sons pursue him thereafter. He does possess Yillah early, mistaking his own superficial pride, youthful iconoclasm, and intuition for blissful revelations of God's and Nature's Truth, but she vanishes when deep thinking brings him doubts. So he pursues her now with philosophical Babbalanja who, like Pani, recognizes the futility of seeking Ultimate Truth and settles, instead, for Christian life on an island. But nothing less than certainty suffices for Taji. He flees on. He seeks self-knowledge through his animal nature with the temptress Hautia; though he seems to glimpse Yillah in man's basic sensuality, he is farther than ever from Truth. It is foolish and futile to seek Truth in man and in this world, so Taji continues his search beyond this world. Yet he would have done better to heed Babbalanja's warning that Yillah will never be found, and that Christian love is of greater value to man than reason.

Newton Arvin
MELVILLE'S MARDI
AQ, II (Spring 1950), 71-81

Although Melville was presented with certain problems in writing *Typee* and *Omoo,* nevertheless he overcame them by drawing upon already established literary forms. In addition, he aimed at expressing experiences which were lacking in complexity and profundity. But during this period Melville matured greatly as a thinker and writer and found himself wanting to probe deeply into the darker areas of the mind. Artistically, he felt the need to express symbolically the growing complexities of his new thinking. His needs were beyond the realm of the romantic narrative, the psychological romance, or the historical novel. Thus he was no longer able to draw upon the mainstream of the nineteenth-century novel but had to seek new forms of expression. *Mardi* was Melville's attempt to achieve new artistic modes, but it is a failure. In it he experiments with several different modes of writing, including the type of novel popularized by Cooper and Marryat, romantic allegory, sentimental symbolism drawing upon the "floral dictionaries" of the period, satire in the manner of Lucian, Rabelais, and Swift, and the legends and myths of Polynesia. Melville's attempt at a mythopoeic amalgamation of Polynesian feeling and imagery, and of the feeling and expression of his own culture, results in failure, but it is significant that he made the attempt. *Mardi* lacks balance as well. It has several centers—intellectual, emotional, political, and social—all of which overlap but do not coalesce. It is a dull novel and an artistic failure, filled as it is with Melville's conflicting emotions, intellectual vacillations, skepticism, and indecision. Nevertheless, as Melville remarks in the novel, "Genius is full of trash," and with all its failings, *Mardi* is still the kind of combination which only genius can achieve.

Nathalia Wright
THE HEAD AND HEART IN MELVILLE'S MARDI
PMLA, LXVI (June 1951), 351-362

In *Mardi*, Melville searches for the fully developed man, the mean between head (ego, acquisitiveness, active aggression, predators, mountain peaks) and heart (senses, sociability, passive retreat, females, valleys). Taji sails from Odo, all head and unsympathetic reason. His first islands alternately contrast heart and head. Valapee destroys ego with infantile intellect; Juam is sensuous, yet inherits usurpation, a head sin; Mondoldo is insensibly sentimental with hearty feasting. Pella dominates with predatory will; Nora-Bamma lusts for divine power; Maramma dictates with tyrannical intellect. Next, head and heart corrupt each other. On Padulla the acquisitive become passively covetous; on Pimminee, head and heart atrophy; on the Isle of Fossils, geology claims that passive senses predate ego; on Diranda killing is a game (heart rejects war and head rejects overpopulation); on Minda heart-poison and head-sorcery destroy social bonds. Then twelve islands show combinations of head-heart dominance in nineteenth-century nations; civilized intellect (mind, not love) dominates primitive emotions. On three others, pretense stifles head and heart. On Serenia, all heart, Odo's (reason's) King Media embraces heart, achieving an historical-cultural—but not metaphysical—mean (for earthly truth is incomplete). Taji seeks complete truth. Rejecting Hautia (aggressive demon) for Yillah (passive deity) and breaking the head-heart (aggression-retreat) division of Mardi's kings, he flees. This is passive-heart retreat, yet also active-head sacrifice. Taji could become fully developed and whole if, like Prometheus, he could actively (head) acquire the sacred fire (Yillah-heart) for mankind.

A. Grove Day
HAWAIIAN ECHOES IN MELVILLE'S MARDI
MLQ, XVIII (March 1957), 3-8

Assuming that *Mardi* has a fictional setting which presents a world of allegory, one still must notice the numerous allusions to the Hawaiian Islands and their customs in the novel. Lahaina, the "village and harbor on the coast of Mowee," is Lahaina, the port on Maui where Melville first debarked. The *Parki* is "bestowed in honor of a high chief, the tallest and goodliest looking in all the Sandwich Islands," a reference to Paki, who was chieftain at the time of Melville's visit. Ohonoo is most likely Oahu, capital of the Hawaiian Islands. Melville's sardonic reference to the "banishing [of] all the objectionable persons to still another island" may have been derived from a specific incident in Hawaiian history in which the chieftains in 1831 expelled the first Catholic missionaries four years after their arrival in Honolulu. The description in Chapter 90 of the approach to Ohonoo resembles the view of the approach to Honolulu as Melville undoubtedly saw it on his arrival in 1843. He could have seen in real life the surfboarding natives described in his novel. Melville was also familiar with William Ellis' *Polynesian Researches During a Residence of Nearly Eight Years in the Society and Sandwich Islands* (1831), and seems to have used this as a basis for surfboarding descriptions and for his reference to the "fifty rebel warriors, driven back into the vale by a superior force," which resembles the Battle of Nuuanu (1795) described by Ellis. The "guardian deities of Mondo" (Chapter 92) are similar to the stone "gods of the Pali" mentioned by Ellis. Other Hawaiian references, such as the fishponds of Mondoldo (Chapter 94), seem to have come from Melville's firsthand observations. Melville in addition relied upon Charles S. Stewart's *A Visit to the South Seas in the U. S. Ship Vincennes* (1831) and also, perhaps, on Stewart's *Journal of a Residence in the Sandwich Islands* (1828, 1839).

Philip Graham

THE RIDDLE OF MELVILLE'S MARDI: A REINTERPRETATION

UTSE, XXXVI (1957), 93-99

The first section of *Mardi* has puzzled critics for many years. Time is the key to understanding the novel, and it is especially in the first section that time becomes the paramount factor. Section one (Chapters 1-62) symbolizes man's prehistoric past and his development; section two (Chapters 63–82) symbolizes man's present; and the third section (Chapter 83 to the end) symbolizes man's future. The journey of the *Chamois* symbolically depicts man's manual and physical development while the journey aboard the *Parki* depicts man's development as a social being. The second journey on the *Chamois* depicts man's spiritual development, wherein he has acquired a conscience and an ideal. The boat is two prowed, and man receives a two-prowed gift that includes an ideal, but also a moral sense of guilt. The middle section of the book portrays man's historic past and describes his present quest for his lost objectives as well as for a moral sense which in turn pursues him. Taji's unwillingness to compromise his moral sense begins the final section, which suggests, inadequately, a journeying out into the unknown waters of the future. This section seems almost to have been included solely to complete a design of Past, Present, and Future, for such a pattern gives the book a unifying theme—man's development through the ages.

REDBURN

(1849)

Willard Thorp
REDBURN'S PROSY OLD GUIDEBOOK
PMLA, LIII (1938), 1146-1156

For factual and dramatic data, Melville often drew on guidebooks. One used in *Redburn,* for the eleven Liverpool chapters, was *The Picture of Liverpool* (1808). Redburn's father, though bankrupt, was a gentleman who once travelled grandly through Liverpool and who gave Redburn this very guidebook. Innocent and proud, Redburn sets out to emulate his father, but times have changed; the book is a deceptive guide, for his Liverpool journey is as disillusioning as his squalid ship's-boy life at sea. It is toward this purpose that Melville uses the guidebook, enlarging on, satirizing, or merely lifting from his source. Simply, he fleshes out the Liverpool chapters by citing data about the city's landmarks, buildings, and docks. Further, he satirizes the prosy old guidebook, mocking its title page, preface, and style for their ornateness, pomposity, and magniloquence. This ridicule of reverent pretense serves Melville's theme, for as Redburn romantically visits his father's hallowed haunts he finds them disappointing or nonexistent. He thinks to visit Riddough's Hotel and the Old Dock and is shocked at time's ravages: they are gone. And his illusions are further shaken. Redburn had dreamed of reliving his father's elegance and so now tries to act with his assurance and flair. One Sunday morning he naively follows his father's steps to a news office, enters like a gentleman, and is met by an attendant. Redburn's squalid clothes receive one perusal. The door slams in his face. His father's guidebook of grand appearances is one thing; reality is something else.

William H. Gilman
MELVILLE'S LIVERPOOL TRIP
MLN, LXI (December 1946), 543-547

Melville's trip to Liverpool formed the substance of *Redburn* (1849). Nineteenth-century biographers, and even Melville's wife, have assigned the date 1837 to the voyage. Modern critics have accepted this date, and on the assumption that Melville was writing autobiography in the novel, have treated episodes and experiences in *Redburn* as though they were Melville's own. A study of a letter by Melville's mother has finally established June 5, 1839, as the correct departure date for the Liverpool trip. The *High-*

lander seems to have been based upon the *St. Lawrence,* a merchant ship which sailed from New York harbor in June, 1839. It departed for Liverpool on June 5 and returned on September 30. That this trip was Melville's maiden ocean voyage is supported by an examination of the ship's official crew list. Thus Melville made his first voyage in 1839, not 1837, as has been supposed. And although he used much autobiographical material in *Redburn,* he also altered the story of his leaving home and taking a job on the *St. Lawrence,* as may be seen by a comparison of Maria Melville's letter with episodes in the novel. Furthermore, he used a young hero imbued with all the characteristics associated with youth. A man of twenty at the time of sailing, and not a boy of seventeen, Melville would have had to be quite immature to have served as the model of Redburn without modifying the character. Thus the critic must be cautious about assuming that Redburn is Melville and the novel his autobiography.

John J. Gross
THE REHEARSAL OF ISHMAEL: MELVILLE'S <u>REDBURN</u>
VQR, XXVII (Autumn 1951), 581-600

Redburn foreshadows much of what later appears in *Moby-Dick,* and allows Ishmael to rehearse the role he will play in that epic. Redburn is an isolatoe like Ishmael, a supersensitive victim of a society not native to him. One of the themes of the novel concerns the situation of the gentleman's son reduced to poor circumstances and isolated from his fellowmen. The novel splits in half and takes a new direction when the ship reaches Liverpool, for at this point Melville shifts his emphasis to social commentary and steps forward as narrator, speaking through a new, mature Redburn. The shift is too abrupt and redirects our attention to the earlier part of the novel, forcing us to realize that Melville's earlier attitude toward his protagonist was indulgent. Redburn never attains a reality beyond his creator's obvious manipulation. He is a passive victim, an innocent who, unlike Billy Budd, lacks the positive force needed in the struggle against evil. He is acted upon rather than acting himself. The novel does not achieve an aesthetic whole. A second theme concerns Redburn's romantic naiveté in his first confrontation with harsh reality. Yet the narrative focus fades in and out and fails to provide a satisfactory total impression. There is a nostalgic quality in some passages which destroys the sense of dramatic immediacy and causes a wrenching of time. Redburn prefigures an archetypal Ishmael who begins with innocence, loses it, and develops an awareness of sin. His return from Liverpool is an archetypal rite of passage, signifying the death of innocence and the rebirth into the world of adult experience.

James Schroeter

REDBURN AND THE FAILURE OF MYTHIC CRITICISM

AL, XXXIX (November 1967), 279-297

Both of the previous modes of interpreting *Redburn* are inadequate or misleading in that they ignore Melville's main organizing feature, his contrast between Jackson and Bolton, and what this contrast implies. The two "previous" modes of interpreting Melville in general are the biographical, which became established in the 1920's, and the mythic, which arose in about 1950. Before the mythic could take hold, the biographical had to be demolished. This was done specifically for *Redburn* by William Gilman's book; and Newton Arvin erected a mythical interpretation on the ruins, claiming that the specific pattern of *Redburn* is to be found in the myth of the "fall of Adam." But this mythic interpretation, although uncritically accepted today, has the same weakness as the biographical interpretation—it does not accurately account for Melville's main pattern. This pattern, like the one in *Moby-Dick* or *Billy Budd,* is made by Melville's contrast between opposite characters—in *Redburn*, between Jackson and Bolton, who represent opposite kinds of experience: American vs. English, plebeian vs. aristocratic, coarse vs. refined, etc. Both have power over Redburn for a time, but both are destroyed, leaving Redburn, the survivor, free and uncommitted. This destruction represents a conscious rejection by Melville of "mythic" and other pre-arranged patterns of experience.*

Terrence G. Lish

MELVILLE'S REDBURN: A STUDY IN DUALISM

ELN, V (December 1967), 113-120

Under duress to relate individual work to system, most critics are misled by general structure into tagging *Redburn* as a tale of initiation of innocence into evil. A closer examination reveals that Melville has inverted the traditional value of the journey symbol. Throughout the novel, the protagonist prudently avoids involvement in evil and, subsequently, denies his brotherhood with mankind. Through the microcosm of the Highlander,

Melville explores the ramifications of dualism by presenting a network of interacting dualities, ranging from schizoid personality to opposing concepts of the universe, one formed by imagination, the other by experience. The Janus-faced captain, the bigamous Max, Redburn and his alter ego, Harry Bolton, the satanic Jackson with his implicit complement, all represent aspects of universal duality on either perceptual or non-perceptual levels. Melville presents a thematic key in Chapter LIII, wherein he expands the "twinning" process to include multiple division and reasserts its extension to ideological worlds. Two sets of "three twins," born to immigrant sisters, all look "as like as . . . figures in a kaleidoscope" so that "together, as well as separately, they seem to form a complete figure." Melville employs the Greek term *Dioscuri* to suggest that Dis and Dios (Satan and God) are but two parts of one entity. In abandoning his intimate friend and benefactor, Harry, penniless in a foreign land, to the good offices of an acquaintance, Redburn denies his brotherhood with mankind, defeats his purpose as seeker, and earns the reader's contempt.*

WHITE-JACKET

(1850)

Keith Huntress
MELVILLE'S USE OF A SOURCE FOR WHITE-JACKET
AL, XVII (1945), 66-74

Professor C. R. Anderson, recognizing that Melville never actually experienced many of the episodes in *White-Jacket*, concludes that they came from his imagination. After all, when Melville wrote the book it had been five years since he had sailed aboard the *United States*. However, Melville himself stated that *White-Jacket* was to be an authentic portrait of life aboard a man-of-war. He drew several of the supposedly imagined episodes from a true account of sea life, *Scenes in "Old Ironsides"* (1841) by a Fore-Top-Man, which includes doggerel poems and sketches. In addition to character names and a verse, Melville borrowed bits of description, dialogue, humorous incidents, and changed them, revealing both his attitude toward the United States Navy of the 1840's and his literary abilities. Whereas *Scenes* exuded uncritical love and praise for officers (favorably contrasted to the drunken sailors), Melville stressed their iniquities, protested floggings, and condemned arbitrary authority. His purpose was to emphasize the brutalities of the Navy, so he exaggerated its negative characteristics. The style in *Scenes* was overblown and immature, but Melville took its best materials and made them interesting. Demonstrating his superior literary skills, he created stinging portraits true to the life that he knew aboard the *United States*.

Howard P. Vincent
WHITE-JACKET: AN ESSAY IN INTERPRETATION
NEQ, XXII (September 1949), 304-315

White-Jacket (1850) represents Melville's uncertain experiment in symbolic fiction and cannot be understood without an examination of its symbolism. Melville's realistic description of the jacket is autobiographical, for he confirmed in a letter that he had himself worn a white jacket while aboard the *United States*. But the jacket is symbolical as well. Melville used white to express ambiguity; it could represent any number of things, including joy, innocence, terror, and emptiness. In *White-Jacket* it is first a symbol of innocence but evolves into one of terror. The jacket provides protection against rough weather and thus has a physical function. White-Jacket desires a self-sufficiency which will help him become aloof from the rest of the crew. The jacket thus symbolizes the protagonist's withdrawal and isolation, as well as his false self-sufficiency. It represents a retreat from the harsher realities of life, an attempt to cling to an innocence almost gone. But the jacket fails him. White-Jacket is nearly killed by his mates when he is mistaken for a ghost. The jacket gradually becomes the object of scorn and ridicule by his shipmates, and their final rejection of the jacket at the auction represents the rejection of its owner as well. White-Jacket's fall from the yardarm is caused by his garment, and symbolizes the Fall of Man and a Christian rebirth. Man must accept all of life, evil as well as good. White-Jacket "dies into life"; his old self is destroyed and a new one born. The book represents Melville's own spiritual growth, disenchantment, and "dying into life." Thus *White-Jacket* is not only literally autobiographical, but is also a description of Melville's own spiritual growth, symbolizing his inner conflicts.

Page S. Procter, Jr.

A SOURCE FOR THE FLOGGING INCIDENT IN WHITE-JACKET

AL, XXII (May 1950), 176-177

Melville invented the flogging incident in *White-Jacket*, concludes Professor C. R. Anderson. The incident shows genteel White-Jacket, mistakenly charged with absence from his post by Captain Claret and sentenced to flogging, madly planning to rush Claret overboard and plunge to death with him. Melville never experienced the incident aboard the *United States,* and Anderson finds no literary analogues for it. But Melville undoubtedly knew of a popular story by William Leggett, "Brought to the Gangway" (1834, 1835), which has the same kind of setting, hero, accusation, sentence, and plunge to death. Leggett tells of gentleman Seaward, shipping aboard a man-of-war as a common sailor, unjustly sentenced to flogging by a sadistic lieutenant and brutal captain for sleeping at his post; after the flogging, Seaward struggles the lieutenant overboard. Melville's version varies from Leggett's in that, while Seaward and the lieutenant drown, White-Jacket's friends stop him and Claret relents. But both versions attack tyrannical naval discipline, a subject receiving sensational exposure in contemporary journals. Melville often used and exaggerated others' experiences to stress naval injustice. Leggett himself tangled with a harsh captain and was forced to leave the navy in 1826, and thus his account perfectly suited Melville's own propagandistic purpose.

Harrison Hayford
THE SAILOR POET OF <u>WHITE-JACKET</u>
BPLQ, III (July 1951), 221-228

Many of the characters in *White-Jacket* were drawn from real-life personalities. Critics have recognized that Williams was modeled after Griffith Williams, a sailor whom Melville probably met in Honolulu. Jack Chase was drawn from John C. Chase of Maine. Nord was patterned after Oliver Russ, who used the name Edward Norton. All three men were real-life friends of Melville's on board the *United States.* A fourth man, "young Lemsford the poet," is not so easily identified, but it is most likely that he was modeled after Ephraim Curtiss Hine. Four years after the cruise, in 1848, Hine published *The Haunted Barque and Other Poems,* twenty of which describe his ocean voyages and ten of which refer to geographical points visited by the *United States.* He continued to publish in popular magazines until 1853, when he went down to a watery grave aboard the *Hamilton.* Two of Hine's poems appearing in *Graham's* were composed at the same time that Hine and Melville were shipmates. One of the poems describes a storm which the *United States* crew weathered off Cape Horn in 1844 and is the same storm depicted in *White-Jacket.* The title of his short novel, *Orlando Melville or the Victims of the Press-Gang, a Tale of the Sea* (1848), suggests that Hine may have been a friend of Melville's. That he contributed regularly to *Gleason's Companion* and that his poems cast light upon Melville's poet are further evidence that Lemsford, the representative of the sailor poet, was undoubtedly modeled after Hine.

TYPEE

(1846)

Russell Thomas
YARN FOR MELVILLE'S <u>TYPEE</u>
PQ, XV (January 1936), 16-29

In writing *Typee,* Melville drew heavily upon Charles Stewart's *A Visit to the South Seas, in the U.S. Ship Vincennes, During the Years 1829 and 1830* (1831). In two volumes, the work devotes all of volume one to a discussion of the Washington Islands, the setting of *Typee.* A comparison of passages from *Typee* and from Stewart's first volume shows that Melville borrowed extensively from that work. In most instances the borrowed material is not a word-for-word reproduction of Stewart but is rather a general borrowing of the whole passage. This comparison also reveals that Melville manipulated his sources to fit his own purposes. Occasionally he borrowed at length without altering the original. Sometimes he altered the original in order to achieve a certain overall mood or feeling, as in "The Encantadas." In some instances, as in *Typee,* Melville seemed to try to cover his tracks in his borrowing. He apparently had Stewart's book before him while composing *Typee,* and must have borrowed from it as he proceeded chapter by chapter. Undoubtedly he used other materials in writing *Typee,* and he has mentioned using several old accounts of Pacific voyages, but it is difficult to discover any other source as influential as Stewart's work. However, there is also a great deal of supporting evidence to show that Melville actually visited Typee Valley and had experiences similar to those described in his book, even to the extent that he, like Tom and Toby, may have at one time been captive of the Typees.

Joseph J. Firebaugh
HUMORIST AS REBEL: THE MELVILLE OF <u>TYPEE</u>
NCF, IX (1954), 108-120

Critics have all too often overlooked a particular, distinguishing quality of Melville's humor: its tolerant geniality. He admires the primitive life while laughing at it and is able to make it the basis of a serious satire on his own civilization. At times he becomes angry, and his humor then is fiercely ironic. But for the most part, his treatment of both the primitive world and his own is suffused with a tolerant geniality. Melville uses a technique of the travel books, the comparison and contrast of the familiar with the unfamiliar, and achieves an incongruous effect by using civilized words for a savage society. For example, he calls the medicine man a "leech," providing ironic commentary on both civilized and savage quackery. His bombastic description of Tom's costume in Typee satirizes the fashions of the civilized world as well as the prose of contemporary fashion magazines. Through the use of incongruity, Melville is able to show the advantages of the savage state over civilized society. He satirizes civilized man by placing him, and his manners, against a background of savage society and shows that human foibles can be found in both worlds. Much of Melville's humor in *Typee* relies upon verbal maneuvering, incongruity, and an ironic juxtaposition of civilized and primitive societies. Using the primitive for a satire upon one's own civilization was no innovation.

Helen B. Petrullo
THE NEUROTIC HERO OF TYPEE

AI, XII (1955), 317-323

D. H. Lawrence has referred to *Typee* as a kind of "birth-myth" and also as an Oedipus myth. It is both. Otto Rank has described the Oedipus myth as an attempt, by Oedipus, in seeking to return to the womb, to solve the riddle of the origin and destiny of man. The hero of *Typee* is concerned with the same attempt. His decision to escape into Typee Valley is a neurotic escape back to the womb after reality has grown too harsh for him. The description of the bay of Nukuheva and the island where the hero wants to flee symbolizes a return to the womb. Hysterical paralysis, says Rank, results from the anxiety associated with the birth trauma. The hero's injured leg immobilizes him, preventing his return to the womb, but it also stops him from overcoming the regression. His vacillations between being drawn to the savages of Typee and the civilized life back home represent what Rank describes as "the 'primal ambivalence' of the psychical." Drawn toward the primitive life in Typee Valley, the hero nevertheless realizes that he is civilized and cannot succumb to savagery. He is at last able to rid himself of his neurotic desire for regression to the womb and escapes on a whale boat. Crushing the head of a Typee pursuer, he frees himself for a return to the open seas of life.

Bartlett C. Jones
AMERICAN FRONTIER HUMOR IN MELVILLE'S TYPEE
NYFQ, XV (Winter 1959), 283-288

Examining the strain of frontier humor in *Typee* can serve to throw some light on the incredulity of Melville's readers when the novel first appeared. His use of understatement, hyperbole, braggadocio, rustic figures of speech, the tall tale, and other devices employed in frontier humor, is one major reason that nineteenth-century readers could not accept the book as an accurate portrayal of life in the South Seas. For example, Melville employs the device of the tall tale when the narrator relates the story of the prolonged voyage of the *Perseverance,* which set out with a crew of young sailors and returned with "twenty Greenwich-pensioner-looking old salts, who just managed to hobble about deck." Melville uses understatement in describing the casualness of Toby in the face of danger, hyperbole in the description of the narrator's stay in Typee Valley, and rustic figures of speech throughout the story. One aspect of American frontier humor involves references to the functions of the human body; eliciting a visceral reaction in the reader are the descriptions of the food on the *Dolly* and the incidents of swallowing live flies and eating raw fish whole. Thus an examination of the thread of frontier humor running throughout *Typee* shows that Melville did not employ the technique as an afterthought and also helps explain the incredulous reactions to the book when it first appeared.

Richard Ruland
MELVILLE AND THE FORTUNATE FALL: TYPEE AS EDEN
NCF, XXIII (December 1968), 312-323

When Melville failed to find a publisher for his first novel, he padded his fiction with anthropological details and persuaded John Murray it was a true travel account. The original implications of the book remain, however, and they can be identified if the narrator's interpretation is separated from the details of the story. Tommo is a deliberate phantast who seeks a primitive paradise and consequently persuades himself that he has found one. But there are moments when he relates without comment, when he seems unaware of the implications of his observations. And he has highly emblematic experiences which are for him wholly without significance. Melville uses Tommo's fear of tattooing, his ailing leg and his suspicion of cannibalism to challenge the value of Typean innocence. The edenic imagery is ironic: for Tommo it connotes happiness, but for Melville it suggests insulation from a necessary exploration of the human condition. Contrary to what Tommo himself seems to assume and his readers to accept, his adventure takes place entirely in the natural sphere. What Tommo finds is indeed unworldly innocence, but it is innocence within the world—the innocence of Baby Budd. Melville's *Typee* can be read as a persuasive indictment of such innocence.*

OMOO

(1847)

Daniel Aaron
MELVILLE AND THE MISSIONARIES
NEQ, VIII (1935), 404-408

Typee and *Omoo* did not find a friendly reception in the South Seas. In *Typee,* Melville lauded the Marquesans, a group previously regarded as savages given to unspeakable practices. Their refusal to be converted by the missionaries further contributed to their unpleasant reputation. Melville condemned the missionaries in *Typee* and directly attacked them in *Omoo.* An examination of certain reviews and articles which appeared in the Honolulu *Polynesian* and the *Friend* between 1846 and 1850 will show the bitter antagonism which Melville and his writing provoked in the South Seas. Most commentators writing about the missionaries approved of their efforts. But a small minority of writers disagreed, suggesting that the missionaries were hypocritical and not entirely motivated by otherworldly aims. They took a Rousseauistic attitude toward the natives, charging that their natural goodness had been depraved by the missionaries. Melville was among this latter group of writers. The earliest references to Melville in the articles of 1846 are generally good-natured. By 1847, however, the commentators had grown more acrimonious. One writer in the *Friend* described Melville as "licentious" and grossly familiar with the "filthy savages of the Marquesas." Nine months later a writer in the *Polynesian* impugned Melville's character in an attempt to disqualify him as an observer of South Sea behavior. In March, 1848, a writer in the *Polynesian* referred to Melville's marriage and suggested a love triangle of Melville, Fayaway, and Melville's bride. Subsequent articles in the *Friend* in the next two years made references to "the dashing Melville" and "the gentle Fayaway," but after a final blast in April, 1850, writers left Melville alone except for a few incidental remarks.

R. S. Forsythe
HERMAN MELVILLE IN TAHITI
PQ, XVI (1937), 344-357
MORE UPON HERMAN MELVILLE IN TAHITI
PQ, XVII (1938), 1-17

Melville's chronology in *Omoo* is somewhat confusing. Sunday, August 14, 1842, seems to be the date on which the *Julia* set sail from the Marquesas. The crew spotted the mountains of Tahiti on the morning of September 20, and that same day mutiny erupted, with Melville and Long Ghost arguing against it. When Consul Wilson boarded the ship to arrest the mutineers, Melville and Long Ghost were also placed in irons. The exact date of Melville's and Long Ghost's departure cannot be definitely determined, but it seems likely they began the journey to Eimeo on November 9. A close examination of sources exterior to *Omoo* corroborates Melville's account of his experiences, and only in a few minor instances does his chronology slip. An English merchant in Tahiti, E. Lucett, in his autobiographical *Rovings in the Pacific* (1851), stated that he was in prison with Melville and Long Ghost and that Melville attacked him with a knife. Evidence points to another person as his attacker, and in fact there is no proof that Melville was in prison at the time of the assault. Lucett seems to have accused Melville because of the latter's unsympathetic portrayal of Dr. Johnston ("Johnson") and Consul Wilson, as well as his unflattering description of the *Julia,* or *Lucy Ann.* Judging from other sources, we see that his handling of the two men is not unnecessarily harsh or unfair and that Lucett's accusations are untenable. Melville employs less fiction than fact in *Omoo*, in contrast to *Typee,* and thus *Omoo* is closer to being an exact autobiography of Melville's adventures in the Marquesas.

Edwin M. Eigner
THE ROMANTIC UNITY OF MELVILLE'S OMOO
PQ, XLVI (1967), 95-108

Omoo has been called a disunified, piecemeal novel (like its name, Tahitian for *wanderer*). Digressions do interrupt the narrator's wanderings, but the unity of *Omoo* is based on theme rather than plot. Image patterns and digressions build a theme of psychological change. Though the narrator's change is gradual, it is complete by the time he meets Dr. Long Ghost. Early, he shudders at Lem Hardy's alienation from home and civilization, but then two digressions reinforce his own, growing alienation. In the first, because of Christian missionaries, the Tahitians are seen as idle, sensual, sick, and alienated from their own country; their social relations, once generous, are now mercenary. In the second digression, the condemned ship *Julia* cruises aimlessly, paralleling the despair of the Tahitians and of the narrator, whom it will neither rescue from alienation nor deliver home. Its crew is alienated, a third having deserted and most of the rest physically and spiritually sick in a comedy of desperation, and sensually degenerate in jail. Completely alienated, the narrator aligns himself with them, wishes to stay in Tamai rather than return home, and dons an outlandish costume of turban and toga. He goes beachcombing with Dr. Long Ghost, a skeptic more alienated than Lem Hardy. In "The Hegira, or Flight," he and the Doctor make their anti-Christian hegira (from *to break off relations*), paralleling Mohammed's flight to Medina. At the end, though crude symbols of home (Christian America) and mother (regeneration) tell of the narrator's return aboard the American *Leviathan,* actions show continuing alienation. Yet despite this contrived ending, *Omoo* is unified in its psychology of despair.

ISRAEL POTTER

(1855)

Roger P. McCutcheon
THE TECHNIQUE OF MELVILLE'S ISRAEL POTTER
SAQ, XXVII (1928), 161-174

Melville used the personal documentary, *The Life and Remarkable Adventures of Israel R. Potter* (1824), as the source of his own *Israel Potter* (1855). The original story is dull, lacks emotion and suspense, and contains little conversation. In his dedication, Melville declares that he has preserved, "almost as in a reprint, Israel Potter's autobiographical story." However, Melville did add original material of his own, comprising approximately two thirds of the novel. Two hundred of the novel's 276 pages are Melville's own additions. Nor did he use all of the material found in the original. Some of his changes consisted of embellishing the original with adventures; others were made to provide character motivation where it seemed lacking in the original. Still others provided plot complications and suspense. Occasionally Melville prepares a scene for the reader; at other times he gives his reader more information about his characters' thoughts and feelings. Whereas in the source the reader is allowed to forget that Potter is an American, Melville stresses his hero's nationality. He achieves a satirical effect with his changes at the end of the novel, when Israel reaches Boston "on a Fourth of July" in 1826. In the original, Israel arrives in June, 1823. This change allows him to gaze at Bunker Hill fifty years after its historic battle. But near the end, the novel borders on melodrama; Melville weakens the ending by departing from the original, which concludes with Israel still alive, and by dwelling on the old man's sorrows and death. It is as if Melville had suddenly tired of his source and wanted to bring the story to a swift conclusion.

Robert M. Farnsworth
ISRAEL POTTER: PATHETIC COMEDY
BNYPL, LXV (1961), 125-132

Israel Potter successfully demonstrates Melville's emergence as a master of irony. To express his beliefs and attitudes Melville couches them ironically in the form of pathetic comedy. Israel Potter engages in one action after another, each time falling back in pathetic defeat. He is a Titan figure, along with John Paul Jones and Ethan Allen, but he is also an archetypal Yankee peddler. In contrast, Benjamin Franklin is a blend of Plinlimmon (*Pierre*) and the Confidence-Man, and is also a complement to John Paul Jones, a blend of poet and outlaw. Just as Melville fearfully suggested in *The Confidence-Man* that America might become the Ben Franklin of nations, assuming a moral code of behavior founded on self-interest, so in *Israel Potter* he suggests that America may become the John Paul Jones of nations. Ironically, Jones captains the *Bon Homme Richard*, and even though he mouths such Franklin aphorisms as "God helps them that help themselves," he does not really believe this to be the case. He has a more poetic, intuitive awareness of the mystery and awe of the universe than does Franklin. The battle between the *Bon Homme Richard* and the *Serapis* is the climax of the book, which ends with prophetic questions reiterated throughout Melville's works: "What separates the enlightened man from the savage? Is civilization a thing distinct, or is it an advanced stage of barbarism?" Thus the novel establishes an ironic tension between what man would like to be and what he really is.

Raymona Hull

LONDON AND MELVILLE'S ISRAEL POTTER

ESQ, XLVII (II Quarter 1967), 78-81

A study of Herman Melville's *Journal of a Visit to London, 1849-1850* shows that he went to London for two purposes: to obtain a British publisher for *White Jacket* and to obtain background material for a novel to be based on a pamphlet, *The Life and Remarkable Adventures of Israel Potter*, supposedly a true story. By comparing episodes from the biographical account with those in the novel the reader sees that Melville changed the tone and scope of the original story by turning a rather sentimental adventure tale into a satire on an American soldier exiled in England after the Revolutionary War. Then by comparing passages from Melville's novel with those from his *Journal* the reader can also understand how Melville reduced to a minimum the gloomy details of Potter's fifty-year exile abroad and used his own recollections as a basis for the few London scenes. In turn he expanded the account of Benjamin Franklin and added a satirical treatment of some other historical personages whom the real Potter never knew. Perhaps during the five years between his departure from London and the writing of *Israel Potter* Melville's bitter experience with criticism of his other publications caused him to produce a lighter piece of fiction than he had originally intended, but one which he thought might please his readers more.*

TALES and SKETCHES

(1856)

Benito Cereno

Max Putzel

THE SOURCE AND THE SYMBOLS OF MELVILLE'S "BENITO CERENO"

AL, XXXIV (May 1962), 191-206

Through Delano's viewpoint, Melville portrays the failure of idealism to cope with primitive reality. Modifying his source (Amasa Delano's *Narrative of Voyages and Travels*), Melville stresses Delano's benign optimism, renames his ship the sexually innocent *Bachelor's Delight*, develops as the story's pattern an appearance-reality tension (Delano's self-assurance prevails despite suspicions of disorder and ambiguity), symbolizes enigmatic primitive power in the slaveship's blacks and Delano's psychology in the ship's approach (it veers, drifts, anchors), contrasts the legal deposition form with psychological evidence and absolute justice, and satirizes reality-blind America. The latter's perceptive intellect and benevolent ideals breed evil, for pure intellect is ultimately blinding, and hence absolute justice leads finally to injustice. Symbolically, intellect ventures into the subconscious *Inferno* and returns ignorant, blinded by commonsensical Virgil. Watching Babo shave Benito, and rushing in fear toward Atufal, Delano senses terror, but intellect blinds him. Benito fails, too. His is the decadent feudal viewpoint, lacking virility, enslaved by hereditary sins. A central figure caught between good-Delano and evil-Babo, Benito flees both father forces and withdraws from life. Beneath Babo's mask of fidelity he glimpses malice, loses faith, and dies. Like Abraham, Delano glimpses disaster, anxiety, guilt and, fearing them, retains his faith. Thus he fails to know what would make him whole—Babo, his forefather, enemy, and virile brother, primitive and barbaric. Good Christian civilization, ignorant of evil, is just as barbaric. It sticks Babo's head on a pole.

Robin Magowan
MASQUE AND SYMBOL IN MELVILLE'S "BENITO CERENO"
CE, XXIII (February 1962), 346-351

Seen in context of the other *Piazza Tales,* "Benito Cereno" presents a ritual action through emblems. Whereas symbols constantly shift meanings, emblems (with fixed meanings) provide formalized unity; they frame the slavery issue (and its appearance-reality problems) with stable moral values. The action is fixed (by Amasa Delano's *Narrative*), and thus the characters are also fixed in unchanging masque roles: Benito is Pathos (cf. saturnalian comedy, the *commedia dell'arte,* Dante's Self-Violent); Delano is a Knight of Civilization (cf. Spenser) surviving evil charms through faith in human decency. Change occurs only in the ritual testing of Delano's faith. It is tested in the slaveship's atmosphere of moral decay, where masquerade contrasts appearance (slavery) with reality (fellowship). Lured by the ship's dark charm, Knight Delano sees a vision of ideal, natural love (Negress), then plunges, lost, into the quarter galley's forest of confusion and falls, grasping for a familiar image. A black-masque saturnalia (the heart of the novella) gives him the image. *The Play of Atufal* parodies slavery, for the key which could unlock Atufal's mock chains ironically chains Benito; the five-knotted rope forces Delano to see the truth of ritual performance. What symbolism makes ambiguous (animal images of enslaved man becoming bestial in a Hobbesian forest, religious images of robed Negroes' sacredness-duplicity tension, black and white slavery symbols becoming gray through Delano's insensitive viewpoint), masque emblems make clear. True to his humane role, though temporarily charmed by his fellowman's slave appearance, Knight Delano passes his ritual test.

David D. Galloway
HERMAN MELVILLE'S "BENITO CERENO": AN ANATOMY
TSLL, IX (Summer 1967), 239-252

The article begins with a review and appraisal of earlier criticism of Melville's novella—particularly that concerned with the author's debt to Captain Amasa Delano's *Voyages and Travels,* and attempts to demonstrate that previous critics have erred in seeing the novella as a whole in terms too easily simplified, no matter how much complexity they might heap upon its individual ingredients. "Benito Cereno" is considered not as allegory or parable, but as a series of reflections on the persistent intermingling of good and evil and a paradigm of the dangers of warped consciousness. Each of the three major characters is bound by codes he has never questioned: Benito Cereno by an effete aristocratic consciousness, Delano by Yankee provincialism, and Babo by the desire for freedom; each approaches the events that Melville records in terms of a rigid preconditioning which makes conventional moral judgements of his behavior untenable. Melville's imagery is analyzed in detail in order to underscore his complex intention and the impressive verbal control which foreshadows his interest in poetry. A careful comparison of "Benito Cereno," one of Melville's most mature and accomplished works, with its source in Delano's *Voyages* is ultimately seen as a way of comprehending Melville's creative techniques as well as the themes which repeatedly concerned him.*

Margaret M. Vanderhaar

A REEXAMINATION OF "BENITO CERENO"

AL, XL (May 1968), 171-191

Melville's works express his concern for American public and social issues, including slavery. Critics of "Benito Cereno" have either ignored the centrality of the slavery problem, or have given widely conflicting opinions on what the story says about the black and white races in America. Melville abhorred slavery and was uncompromisingly convinced that the South was wrong in the Civil War, although he mitigated his blame of Southerners by saying that they were only the inheritors, not the originators, of slavery. However, in "Benito Cereno" he portrays the slaves and their leader Babo as brutal, violent, destructive savages, characteristics which Captain Delano wholly fails to comprehend. The well-meaning innocent captain cherishes a fatuous patronizing view about Negroes (to him they are excellent servants and cheerful harmless primitives) which ignores their human capacity for evil and resentment of enslavement. It seems at first that order, justice and kindness are prerogatives of the white Europeans and Americans, while the Africans evince no capacity except for anarchy, violence and deceit. But in reality one principle animates both races: might makes right. When the revolt is subdued, the whites deal with the slaves as barbarously as they had dealt with their white masters. The ship's stern-piece, bearing the arms of Spain and depicting a masked satyr with his foot on the neck of a writhing figure, also masked, symbolizes the story's meaning. Slavery originated in the Old World, but Delano the archetypal American is the satyr, half man, half beast (recurrent animal imagery suggests the brutalizing dehumanizing effects of slavery on both master and slave). His benevolent mask hides a moral vacuum, while the writhing figure wears a mask of subservience that hides a resentment so ferocious that it erupted into the bloody revolt aboard ship. "Benito Cereno" suggests that slavery is the snake in the American Garden of Eden which later caused the Civil War and ensuing difficulties for the coexistence of the two races.*

Bartleby

Egbert S. Oliver

A SECOND LOOK AT "BARTLEBY"

CE, VI (May 1945), 431-439

In his withdrawal from a society he despises, Bartleby portrays not
Melville but Thoreau. He is a *reductio ad absurdum* of Thoreau's *Civil
Disobedience* and *Walden.* Thoreau found organized society unprincipled,
refused it his allegiance, and withdrew into solitude. Like Thoreau, who
copied Emerson, Bartleby quietly sat behind a screen copying his master's
work. Thoreau declined to pay taxes, and Bartleby preferred not to copy
anymore. Others had to supply their needs (office space, and Emerson's
property where Thoreau squatted) and do their mundane work. Giving no
reasons, they stood aloof from society in passive noncooperation, Bartleby
gazing out his office window in solitude, just as Thoreau gazed from his
prison. They believed prison was where they should be, since the state was
unprincipled. As Thoreau said, man must depend on and live within himself alone. Thoreau's jailors were just as bewildered about him as were
Bartleby's associates; though Thoreau and Bartleby could shun society,
society could not be rid of them and considered them eccentric for sever-
ing all human ties. Though Melville often sympathized with Bartleby, just
as he admired Thoreau's heroic stubbornness, he found this self-reliance and
aloof individualism absurd. To prefer to live solely within oneself is to stop
living; Bartleby shriveled up until he ceased to be a man. His loneliness
overwhelmed his employer, the narrator; indeed, if any character
portrayed Melville it was the narrator, for through him Melville mused
about the kind of loneliness that he himself experienced at Arrowhead.
"Bartleby" reveals Melville's interest in his literary contemporaries and his
continuing analysis of man and society. And in its satire of Thoreau, it
reveals Melville's wholesome sanity.

Norman Springer

"BARTLEBY" AND THE TERROR OF LIMITATION

PMLA, LXXX (1965), 410-418

The terrible revelation of "Bartleby" is that the narrator, with his complex intellectual abilities, is unable to know the heart's limitations. His pride, his optimism and worldly ethic, his mastery over men (in terms of orderliness, prudence, detachment), and his confidence that with his respectable, practical abilities he can cope with Bartleby all fail. Because he senses failure, he deserves respect; because he strives to go beyond his customary outlook, he becomes less predictable and creates an atmosphere of suspense. He just might succeed. He tries pity, yet he fears to pity Bartleby, to identify with terror, to find his fundamental optimism destroyed, and thus to know that his own inability to pity and to deal with evil is not unique, but universal. Suffering a sense of moral limitation, he tries to regain equilibrium with Christian charity. But charity fails, for behind Christianity's mask lurk paganism and the vacant wall (Wall Street, office, Bartleby) which charity cannot endure. Thus, falling back on pride, self-esteem, and *assumptions,* the lawyer screens himself from this pagan void and from Bartleby's *preference.* Bartleby prefers to withdraw from the world, for to acknowledge death and to see man's moral failure in life (his incapacity for compassion) are to realize the meaninglessness of all action and belief. His withdrawal is terrible, but the narrator's is worse. Pulling back from the void of what *is* to the illusion of what *should be,* he relies on dead letters and on a purblind optimism that, somehow, he has successfully classified Bartleby. The terror is that he turns from heart to head, imagines that he finds meaning in the incomprehensible, and with this illusion hides from the terrible limitation of his heart.

Herbert F. Smith

MELVILLE'S MASTER IN CHANCERY AND HIS RECALCITRANT CLERK

AQ, XVII (1965), 734-741

The narrator's position—Master in Chancery—is the guiding metaphor in "Bartleby." The ancient English Courts of Chancery, the King's conscience, judged both legality *and* morality. Called Courts of Equity (concerned with absolute justice, the spiritual-ideal), they differed from

Courts of Common Law (concerned with relative justice, the material-real). The existence of both courts in America suggested to Melville a monarchy-democracy division, which he analyzed in his story's law-office microcosm. The narrator was formerly a pettifogger, unambitious and inexperienced in law, safe and content in his practical, common-law view-point. Ironically, he is made Master in Chancery, now obliged to strive for ideal justice. The two concepts of law contradict in principle and conflict in him. Enter Bartleby, his double. Hired for practical reasons, he behaves practically, mirroring the narrator's common-law mentality. Then the narrator, becoming Equity conscious, calls copying dull, whereupon Bartleby prefers not to copy, becoming spiritually recalcitrant. So goes the story. As the narrator faces unimagined complexities and ambiguities in his growth toward Equity, Bartleby presents him with cases in point. He stresses *prefer,* the key to Equity law (which, vs. common-law pleading, considers plaintiff preference); here Melville stresses man's existential choice. At last the narrator abandons his common-law literalness with Bartleby and embraces ideal charity (full Equity), restoring equilibrium to his microcosm on this spiritual plane. But practical, social-material pressures compromise him and kill his Chancery-awareness—Bartleby—who must seek Equity in Heaven, for on earth, spiritual and material justice remain unreconciled.

Peter E. Firchow

BARTLEBY: MAN AND METAPHOR

SSF, V (Summer 1968), 342-348

At the end of "Bartleby," the narrator mentions "one vague report" which reached him some months after Bartleby's death concerning the latter's former employment in the dead-letter office in Washington, D. C. This additional information is crucial to the story as a whole, and in fact, everything in the story leads up to it. Bartleby is metaphorically a dead letter which has been sent the narrator and which apparently contains an important message, although the narrator has no assurance that the "letter" is either addressed to him or contains an important message. The story depicts the failure of communication. The narrator is qualified, as a "conveyancer and title hunter, and drawer up of recondite documents of all sorts," to decipher such a "recondite document." Rationality is his major characteristic, and his failure to deal with Bartleby and the latter's irrational behavior represents his inability to "read" him, for he is "writ-ten" in a "language" which the narrator cannot comprehend. Ultimately the narrator realizes he must accept Bartleby as he is, but doing so would necessarily embarrass him professionally. Lacking the courage to evict Bartleby, the narrator vacates his office and, in so doing, metaphorically refuses to accept his human letter and leaves no "forwarding address." The Tombs represents the dead-letter office where Bartleby, the "dead letter," must die. Bartleby is ultimately destroyed because he lacks the common-sense qualities of the narrator and has allowed himself to suffer irrationally from the pity brought on by his experiences in the dead-letter office. As Ishmael says, "There is a wisdom that is woe; but there is a woe that is madness." Melville's story stresses the human condition; rather than merely indicting society, it depicts the isolation of man and his inability to communicate with his fellowman. It is the additional information about Bartleby we are given at the end that contributes significantly to this emphasis and to making the story an aesthetically integrated whole.

Miscellaneous

Merton M. Sealts

HERMAN MELVILLE'S "I AND MY CHIMNEY"

AL, XIII (1941), 142-154

Like *Pierre* (1852), "I and My Chimney" (1855) allegorizes Melville's fear of hereditary insanity, a fear stemming from his father's having died insane. After *Moby-Dick* (1851), Melville's health suffered, and by 1853 his mother, aware of her son's concern with his father's insanity in *Pierre,* called doctors to examine Melville's own sanity. In "I and My Chimney," Melville warns against probing the heart and soul too deeply. The narrator's wife seeks to remove their chimney, calls a master stonemason to examine it and, hearing his report of a possible secret chamber in the chimney, suspects the narrator's kinsman, Dacres, of hiding treasure there when he built the house. Fighting her efforts to probe the chimney's secret, the narrator pays the mason to certify the chimney's soundness and refuses to surrender it to further examination. Altering historical facts, Melville has portrayed his father as Dacres, the kinsman, whose name is an anagram of "sacred," and has portrayed his critical, nagging mother as the wife. Paralleling identical concerns and images in *Pierre,* the chimney allegorizes body and soul in its labyrinthine architecture, bottomless shaft, and sacred pyramid. To probe it too deeply is to violate sacred memories (of father) and to cripple one's own fortitude—and sanity. The narrator (Melville) will not surrender his house's backbone. The doctors, of course, pronounced Herman Melville completely sane. What is remarkable is that, far from offering a mere description of his farmhouse at Arrowhead, Massachusetts, Melville once again offers to public view a deep analysis of his own profound, personal problems.

Charles A. Fenton
"THE BELL-TOWER": MELVILLE AND TECHNOLOGY
AL, XXIII (May 1951), 219-232

Melville condemns technology in "The Bell-Tower." The Renaissance setting parallels New England of the 1850's with its dreadful finance capitalism and new technology of locomotives, machine-producing machines, and assembly lines. As in "The Tartarus of Maids," brutalizing industrialism replaces and imprisons man, subordinating him to utilitarianism; as in Hawthorne's "Ethan Brand," Benthamistic pride in unlimited human progress through reason is destructive. Like Ahab, Bannadonna the mechanician asserts his absolute self-sufficiency. A picture of vanity, his bell-tower rises ominously over the trees. He vaunts his mastery over nature and, in physical achievements, his equality with the other Creator. But he does not act alone. Participation is a central theme of the story. The whole populace shares his crime, conspiring to elevate man as they ceremoniously gather at the tower on holy days (evoking factory-cornerstone and railway-linking ceremonies) and succumb to the charm of the pagan clock-bell. All adulate the proud mechanician—the proletariat, petty bureaucracy, and nobility. Finally, they participate in the death of their most robust countryman as the pagan bell re-hung in the cathedral falls, in Bannadonna's stately funeral, and in the repair of the broken tower. Their guilt is clear. Nature destroys the tower with an earthquake, but Bannadonna destroys himself. American man seeks stability in the very science that dislocates him, but rationality, pragmatism, and materialism destroy sympathy for man; the triumphant bell, flawed by blood, crushes Bannadonna's brain. Technology threatens that which sustains man—his responsibility to his fellowman and to God.

Charles G. Hoffmann
THE SHORTER FICTION OF HERMAN MELVILLE
SAQ, LII (July 1953), 414-430

Written at the height of Melville's success, following the triumph of *Moby-Dick, Pierre* demonstrates the collapse of his romance method. Both novels presented him with similar problems, for both lack a central, unifying structure. *Moby-Dick,* however, is successful because it has epic grandeur, and its rhetoric and characterization sustain the narrative. But in

Pierre the rhetoric overpowers the characters. The novel fails as well in its lack of a unifying structure and point of view. Both novels presented Melville with the problem of working with large pieces of material and thus tend to break down into shorter narrative units. The short novel and short story were Melville's forte, however, for their necessary economy did away with elaborate rhetoric, providing him with the means of achieving organic unity by using a single block of material. "Bartleby the Scrivener" (1853) displays Melville's mastery of his material. In contrast to the technique of *Moby-Dick* and *Pierre*, in which he tries to achieve complexity through an expanded, elaborate rhetoric, in "Bartleby" he employs a simple, economical language which conveys complexity of meaning. "Cock-A-Doodle-Do!" represents Melville's further experimentation with short fiction, as does "The Encantadas" (1854). His publications in 1855, such as "Benito Cereno," reveal his growing competence in handling shorter forms of prose fiction. Thus, although Melville employs a rather exaggerated style in *Moby-Dick* and *Pierre,* in his subsequent short stories and novels he seems to return to the simple, natural style characteristic of his earlier writing. "Bartleby" represents the beginning of Melville's achievement of the discipline of a tighter form, a more economical language, and a nice balance between theme and technique. He matured as an artist through his experimentation with short prose fiction, and one can only regret that he was unable to apply his new skills to the full-length novel form.

W. R. Thompson

"THE PARADISE OF BACHELORS AND THE TARTARUS OF MAIDS": A REINTERPRETATION

AQ, IX (Spring 1957), 34-45

Critics usually separate the stories, studying sex or industrial evils in "Maids" (missing its sex-machine satire) and calling "Bachelors" a glutton's revel or monkish retreat from evil. Melville links them. Both Old World gentility and American industrialism are spiritually sterile. White imagery in "Maids" is virginal, innocent, yet barren and coldly impersonal; similarly ambiguous is black imagery in "Bachelors," idyllic and solemn, yet sequestered from the active world. The bachelors, degenerate shadows of the virile Knights-Templars, priest-soldiers who fought chivalrously for human welfare, ironically dote on banquet skirmishes and scholarly trivia, pooh-pooh misery, and impotently fill the Templar's phallic horn with snuff; they fail their responsibility to man. Similarly, blind to misery, the mill manager in "Maids" dotes on industrial production; his humanism impotent, he enslaves his robot girls, sacrificing man to machine. England is the placid Thames and grave Socrates, coldly codified; America is the raging, wasteful Blood River and innocent Cupid, bound in expediency, babyblind to cruelty. The seedsman-narrator, who observes both worlds, represents paternalism and responsibility toward man. Yet his seeds (human vitality) are machine-packaged and carry industrialism westward, just as the mill's rags (the world's human materials) are pressed into conformity. Each world needs but lacks the other's strength—Europe's theoretical humanism, America's vital pragmatism. Both worlds, spiritually stunted, show (like Captain Delano in "Benito Cereno") an impotent disregard for human values.

Alvin Sandberg

EROTIC PATTERNS IN "THE PARADISE OF BACHELORS AND THE TARTARUS OF MAIDS"

L&P, XVIII (1968), 2-8

A study of the structure, imagery and symbolism of "The Paradise of Bachelors and the Tartarus of Maids" leads to the conclusion that Melville is portraying an impotent seedman who prefers the masturbatory paradise of the Temple because his dream vision of the Black Notch—heterosexual contact—is a frightening one indeed. He visits the effete bachelors to discover that their lives are happy and prosperous because they have eschewed the entanglements of matrimony: they do not worry about "the rise of bread and fall of babies." The imagery used to describe their retreat is consistently oral, as is their excessive pre-occupation with food. Masturbatory and vaguely homosexual, life at the Temple is the seedman's safe haven away from demanding heterosexuality. The second half of the diptych is a dream vision in which all the seedman's fears are symbolically represented. The paper mill of the Black Notch—the vagina—is the seedman's childish conception of coitus, with maidens tending upright, knife-like shafts that shred rag paper. His castration, or fear of it, is apparent in his limp and in his horse's condition after they leave the notch; the animal is "all cringing and doubled up with the cold." Cupid and Old Batch may be father figures who are concerned with the opportune "withdrawal" of the seedman, and the seedman may be the young boy who feels threatened by the sexually overbearing father; but the story does not offer enough clues to substantiate completely such an interpretation. As the seedman cries, "Carry me back to old Virginny," back to adolescent and infantile sexlessness and away from the demands of adult heterosexuality.*

Paul Deane

HERMAN MELVILLE: FOUR VIEWS OF AMERICAN COMMERCIAL SOCIETY

RLV, XXXIV (1968), 504-507

In four short stories (three virtually ignored by critics), Melville examines the extent to which commercialism thwarts and enslaves the human spirit. "The Paradise of Bachelors and the Tartarus of Maids" considers the world of assembly-line production, wherein all personality and individualism become absorbed into the work. The factory in the Tartarus section is a whitewashed building located in a white hollow; the workers are blank-looking girls folding blank, white paper—empty people without a life beyond their work. The titular character in "Bartleby the Scrivener" has an equally limited life—the view from his office window being "the white wall of a spacious skylight shaft." As the story develops, he comes never to leave the office. A copyist, he originates nothing, and like the assembly-line girls in "Tartarus," his life is a series of repetitive and meaningless actions. "Jimmy Rose" presents a wealthy and socially prominent man whose "friends" desert him when he loses his money. Jimmy is reduced to subservience and forced to crawl for food at the homes of former associates. He can bear the humiliation because he values only social position and money, elements that have beguiled many Americans. Finally, "The Fiddler" examines the place to which the artist is reduced in a commercial society: the safest course is to suppress one's genius and become a teacher or a clown. These are acceptable and accepted roles. The pure artist-genius is an anomaly.*

Helmbrecht Breinig

THE DESTRUCTION OF FAIRYLAND: MELVILLE'S "PIAZZA" IN THE TRADITION OF THE AMERICAN IMAGINATION

ELH, XXXV, No. 2 (June 1968), 254-283

"The Piazza" demonstrates Melville's views on range and limits of the artistic imagination and the possibilities of art as epistemology, and his method of trying out the values of ideas by putting them into action. For this complex purpose, he placed his work in a literary tradition going back to the European Romanticists who had used fairy-tale imagery in order to give their works the temporally/spatially remote settings necessary for the fictional representation of spiritual struggles. The discrepancy between their ideals and anti-fiction actuality led American writers from Irving onwards to create similar realms of the imagination as bases for their writings. Following this tradition, we find Hawthorne's "Old Manse" an interesting example as it shares the complex introductory function with his romance-prefaces and indicates the symbolical process by which truth in his sense can be found in a "neutral territory." Textual parallels reveal that "The Piazza" copies fairy-setting and introductory function. However, by putting Hawthorne's ideas into a symbolic narrative action, Melville makes his work a fictional test of Hawthorne's "truth" and of his artistic achievement. The fairlyland-metaphor and along with it the more optimistic ideas in Hawthorne's sketch as well as some of Thoreau's are reduced to absurdity. As the multiple symbolical action of "The Piazza" shows, disillusionment is the fate of all romantic idealists. In Melville's view, the destruction of the imaginative realm in which other American authors had hoped to find a solution to their artistic problems is necessary for the development of art.*

POETRY

(1866-1891)

Newton Arvin
MELVILLE'S SHORTER POEMS
PR, XVI (October 1949), 1034-1046

Following the period in which Poe, Emerson, and Whitman wrote, American poetry took two directions. The first, anticipated by Poe and Whitman and taken by Sidney Lanier, was symbolically indirect, musical, incantatory. The other, anticipated by Emerson and taken by Emily Dickinson, was colloquial, prosaic, anti-poetic, and ironic. Melville also took this path and was, in a sense, a precursor of a whole line of twentieth-century American poets. Melville disliked the early romantic language and rhetoric and was unhappy with the dream world of romantic idealism. Like Hardy, he insisted on a "rendering of the Real," and was determined to show the many sides of reality. Thus his poetry avoids conventional romantic diction and instead demonstrates a prosaic, but powerful, language with terms suggestive of industry, the law, business, and mathematics. Melville does not rely upon rarities or nonce words in achieving verbal impact, for he displays the true poet's native command of language through use of a familiar word in such a way that it suddenly seems to bear a magic potency. At times he uses words to convey irony or produce a strange connotative meaning. He employs striking imagery, including astronomical, meteorological, geographical, geological, nautical, naturalistic, and elemental images. Although most of his poems are imperfect, nevertheless some exhibit such a union of thought and feeling, of form and content, that it is foolish to regard them as amateurish. Melville's verse reveals an autumnal attitude in which he repudiates the "juvenile and shallow" exuberance and hopefulness of his age, yet also rejects the unqualified negativism of a Mark Twain or a Henry Adams.

Walter E. Bezanson
MELVILLE'S CLAREL: THE COMPLEX PASSION
ELH, XXI (1954), 146-159

Clarel is a complex work of imagination with a symbolic situation and site. Out of the six main locations emerge reflections on theology, history, and psychology, all of which sustain the poem. In Part I, the Holy City is revealed as a Fallen City and Clarel as a lost hero in pursuit of a spiritual guide. This spiritual search forms a major pattern of the poem.

The Night Journey occurs in Part II, in which the pilgrims begin their symbolic descent. "Prelusive" and "Sodom" carry Part II to a climax. The Dead Sea signifies the danger of annihilation, total evil, and the intolerable boundaries of introspection. "Mar Saba," Part III, is analogous to Dante's Purgatorio, as the pilgrims leave the site of absolute evil. By the end of Part III both Mortmain and Nehemiah, potential guides for Clarel, are dead. Mortmain's complex passion and Nehemiah's simple goodness do not provide Clarel with a pattern to follow, and in Part IV he begins to copy Rolfe's language and views. Clarel's spiritual state at Mar Saba is echoed by the Wilderness. Longing for rebirth, but denied it, he finds himself "*'Suspended 'twixt the heaven and hell.'*" In Part IV the pilgrims travel on to Bethlehem. Clarel is now drawn toward two new extremes, celibate asceticism and apostasy. He enters "The Valley of Decision" and arrives back at the "complex passion" which he had experienced earlier at the Holy Sepulcher. He now knows this complexity through experience and recognizes fresh problems of limitless complexity. The poem tells us that they can neither be escaped nor solved. Earlier, Clarel had hoped to win Ruth and enter Paradise, but despair and suffering are his, as he arrives at a tragic view of life in which he cannot escape the Passion. As he sees Eden transformed into Gethsemane, his initiation rites are completed.

Laurence Barrett

THE DIFFERENCES IN MELVILLE'S POETRY

PMLA, LXX (September 1955), 606-623

Melville's poetry wrenches form and meaning violently, but these wrenchings, or *differences* (poetic devices), are not flaws; they effectively express Melville's world view. They evolved as he struggled to reconcile art with life. He first thought poetry distinct from philosophy and shunned its forms for philosophy's deep, intellectual insight. In *Typee* he sought Absolute Truth through allegory, with its intellectual, one-to-one equation of image with feeling. From *Mardi* to *Moby-Dick,* as he struggled to reconcile heart (felt symbol, experience) with head (intellectualized symbol, thought), he progressed from allegory to a symbolism rich with multiple meanings and ambiguities (which deny absolutes). Melville found that poetry and philosophy merge (become identical, not distinct) in the process of creating symbolism, that he could reconcile heart and head through poetic *form,* and that measured form itself is creative, making undeniably real what the heart feels but the head finds ambiguous. Thus evolved his three *differences:* his highly personal feeling-symbols (often unnoticed, or seemingly trite); his violent yoking of divergent ideas (reflecting ambiguity, a metaphor stresses one meaning and simultaneously denies it); his conflicts of form (clashing rhymes, meters, stanza forms) expressing contrasting, changing ideas. Along with his concept of poetic form (epitomized in *Billy Budd*), these *differences* occur in Melville's prose, illuminate his novelistic techniques, and raise his stature as a poet. Thinking life formless, Melville had rebelled against form. Though he found through his reverence for Greek architecture and archetypes that in form art endures, to mirror life, he was forced to wrench form.

Gene B. Montague
MELVILLE'S BATTLE-PIECES
UTSE, XXXV (1956), 106-115

Many of the poems in *Battle-Pieces* (1866) exhibit problems with unity, diction, imagery, and meter. They disappoint us mainly because they represent the juvenile phase of Melville's development as an artist. However, some poems in the collection reveal a refreshing awareness not found in the poetry of many of Melville's contemporaries. For example, "The Portent" (1859) displays an increasing concentration of image, while "Malvern Hill" (July 1862) reveals Melville's command of diction. And although he often had trouble with meter, in "The House-Top" (July 1863), tempo has been skillfully fitted to mood. Viewed against the backdrop of Melville's pacifist philosophy, expressed in his earlier works, *Battle-Pieces* at first seem to repudiate his earlier views or suggest his confusion on the matter. Neither case is correct. In "Misgivings" (1860) Melville writes that war is degrading because it subordinates man's sublime nature to barbarism. He sees the Civil War as growing out of the same tragic, paradoxical mixture of good and evil which pervades his earlier writing. Although *Battle-Pieces* are pro-Union, and although Melville stood on the side of the North, nevertheless he felt that wholly blaming any one group for the war was impossible. He saw both Southern and Northern soldiers as innocent pawns in a war for which they were not really responsible. Thus there is in *Battle-Pieces* no sharp distinction between Northern and Southern soldiers. Rather, the poems ask the questions of whether the price man must pay for even a partial victory over evil may not be too great, whether this price may not itself become an evil, and whether the joy of victory may not conflict with good.

Richard Harter Fogle
MELVILLE'S <u>CLAREL</u>: DOUBT AND BELIEF
TSE, X (1960), 101-116

Clarel is in many ways magnificent, but it lacks unity and development. The pilgrimage motif does not blend with the love motif. The real conflicts in the poem are between ideas, not living characters capable of change or development. The theme concerns religious doubt. Clarel is confronted with the presence of evil as the dominant force in life. Nehemiah blindly relies upon Scripture while failing to see evil. Derwent constantly ignores the unpleasant and looks only for the agreeable side of life. Rolfe is the opposite, and is in part similar to Melville. Learned, experienced, cosmopolitan, he doggedly pursues all philosophical questions regardless of where they may lead, even to the brink of nihilism. Just as Rolfe is in part Melville, so Vine is reminiscent of Hawthorne. He represents a duality of darkness and light, sensualism and asceticism, reticence and warmth. He is both innocent and partaker of some mysterious darkness beyond mere sinfulness. Mortmain and Ungar are alienated from the world, Mortmain representing fallen man of the Old World, Ungar, fallen man of the New. Inasmuch as both believe in supernaturalism but lack the comfort of a specific credo, the two represent Melville. *Clarel* does not resolve doubt or arrive at a definite conclusion. The Epilogue summarizes Melville's argument, revealing the dualism of his thinking. He rejects pantheism as well as the idea that God or man is capable of evolutionary growth. While he views fallen man's mixed nature and the unwillingness of God to intervene in man's existence as evidence of the dualism and strife that are the legacy of mankind, still Melville believes that man cannot survive without faith.

Darrell Abel
"LAUREL TWINED WITH THORN": THE THEME OF MELVILLE'S <u>TIMOLEON</u>
Person, XLI (July 1960), 330-340

One theme is reiterated throughout the poems in *Timoleon* (1891) which unifies them into a work of art—the idea that intellectuals and artists are alienated from their fellowmen by their innovative, nonconformist thinking. The title poem, "Timoleon," suggests that, like

Timoleon, Melville felt he had been isolated from his fellowmen by his transcendence over the ordinary. Timoleon is torn by conflicting loyalties to his family and to his country, but in assassinating his brother he displays a transcendent loyalty to his country. Melville himself was torn between loyalty to himself and loyalty to his public. In turning away from the popular, romantic fiction exemplified by *Typee* and *Omoo* and concerning himself in *Pierre* and *Moby-Dick* with metaphysical and moral questions which alienated his audience, Melville displayed a transcendent loyalty to his own vision of truth. "After the Pleasure Party" assesses the cost of such transcendence. Urania discovers to her sorrow that transcendence is purchased at the expense of the enjoyment of life. "The Night-March," "The Margrave's Birthnight," and "The Garden of Metrodorus" all deal with the third aspect of the theme of intellectual alienation—the idea that the lives of great men are unreal and incomprehensible to ordinary men. "After the Pleasure Party," "Lamia's Song," and "The Bench of Boors" show the longings of the alienated intellectual for the world of ordinary men. "Lamia's Song," as well as "Shelley's Vision," "C's Lament," "Monody," and "In a Garret" are also concerned with the idea that the alienated genius may be estranged from his fellowmen, yet belongs to a timeless community of great men.

Jane Donahue

MELVILLE'S CLASSICISM: LAW AND ORDER IN HIS POETRY

PLL, V (Winter 1969), 63-72

The tension in Melville's mind between a desire for freedom and a countervailing impulse toward order, although evident in his fiction, appears most clearly in his poems dealing with classical themes. The travel poems of *Timoleon* reveal a deep respect for the harmonious relationship of nature, man, and art expressed in Greek architecture and aesthetic theory. Although Melville looked upon the classical cultures as the highest development of personal and social character, he recognized in "The House Top" that social order depends on law rather than on human nature which, when unrestrained, slips into the romantic primitivism of "Syra" or descends to bestiality. He was attracted to the apparent repose of classical civilization but warned in "The Age of the Antonines" against the attempt to escape modern problems by a return to the past. The strong appeal of classical order, stasis, and impersonality to a man essentially as romantic as Melville suggests that he, like Byron, may have sought in Greek and Roman art some outer principle of order to control his own basically lawless imagination.*

Finding List of Periodicals

AI	*American Imago*
AL	*American Literature*
AQ	*American Quarterly*
ArQ	*Arizona Quarterly*
AS	*American Speech*
ATQ	*American Transcendental Quarterly*
BNYPL	*Bulletin of the New York Public Library*
BPLQ	*Boston Public Library Quarterly*
BSUF	*Ball State University Forum*
CD	*Comparative Drama*
CE	*College English*
ELH	*Journal of English Literary History*
ELN	*English Language Notes*
ES	*English Studies*
ESQ	*Emerson Society Quarterly*
KR	*Kenyon Review*
L&P	*Literature and Psychology*
MassR	*Massachusetts Review*
MLN	*Modern Language Notes*
MLQ	*Modern Language Quarterly*
MQR	*Michigan Quarterly Review*
NCF	*Nineteenth-Century Fiction*
NEQ	*New England Quarterly*
NYFQ	*New York Folklore Quarterly*
Person	*Personalist*
PLL	*Papers on Language and Literature*
PMLA	*Publications of the Modern Language Association*
PQ	*Philological Quarterly*
PR	*Partisan Review*
PrS	*Prairie Schooner*
RLV	*Revue des Langues Vivantes*
RS	*Research Studies*
SAQ	*South Atlantic Quarterly*
SR	*Sewanee Review*
SSF	*Studies in Short Fiction*
TSE	*Tulane Studies in English*
TSLL	*Texas Studies in Literature and Language*

UKCR	*University of Kansas City Review*
UTSE	*University of Texas Studies in English*
VQR	*Virginia Quarterly Review*
YR	*Yale Review*

Bibliography

Biographical Studies

Anderson, Charles R. *Melville in the South Seas.* New York: Columbia University Press, 1939.

Arvin, Newton. *Herman Melville.* New York: William Sloane Associates, 1950. Reprint. New York: Viking Press, Compass Books, 1957.

Gilman, William H. *Melville's Early Life and Redburn.* New York: New York University Press, 1951.

Howard, Leon. *Herman Melville: A Biography.* Berkeley: University of California Press, 1951.

Leyda, Jay. *The Melville Log: A Documentary Life of Herman Melville, 1819-1891.* 2 vols. New York: Harcourt, Brace, 1951.

Metcalf, Eleanor Melville. *Herman Melville: Cycle and Epicycle.* Cambridge: Harvard University Press, 1953.

Mumford, Lewis. *Herman Melville: A Study of His Life and Vision.* Rev. ed. New York: Harcourt, Brace & World, 1962.

Sealts, Merton M., Jr. *Melville as Lecturer.* Cambridge: Harvard University Press, 1957.

Weaver, Raymond. *Herman Melville, Mariner and Mystic.* New York: Cooper Square Publishers, 1921.

Scholarship and Criticism

Books

Baird, James R. *Ishmael: A Study of the Symbolic Mode in Primitivism.* Baltimore: Johns Hopkins University Press, 1956. Reprint. New York: Harper & Row, Harper Torchbooks, 1960.

Bernstein, John. *Pacifism and Rebellion in the Writings of Herman Melville.* The Hague: Mouton, 1964.

Berthoff, Warner. *The Example of Melville.* Princeton: Princeton University Press, 1962.

Bowen, Merlin. *The Long Encounter: Self and Experience in the Writings of Herman Melville.* Chicago: University of Chicago Press, 1960.

Braswell, William. *Melville's Religious Thought: An Essay in Interpretation.* Durham, N.C.: Duke University Press, 1943. Reprint. New York: Pageant Books, 1950.

Brodtkorb, Paul, Jr. *Ishmael's White World: A Phenomenological Reading of "Moby Dick."* New Haven: Yale University Press, 1965.

Canaday, Nicholas, Jr. "A New Reading of Melville's 'Benito Cereno,'" in

Studies in American Literature, eds. Waldo McNeir and Leo B. Levy. Baton Rouge: Louisiana State University Press, 1960, 49-57.

Dahlberg, Edward. *"Moby-Dick:* An Hametic Dream," in *Varieties of Literary Experience,* ed. Stanley Burnshaw. New York: New York University Press, 1962, 183-213.

Davis, Merrell R. *Melville's Mardi: A Chartless Voyage.* New Haven: Yale University Press, 1952. Reprint. Hamden, Conn.: Shoe String Press, 1967.

Finkelstein, Dorothee Metlitsky. *Melville's Orienda.* New Haven: Yale University Press, 1961.

Fogle, Richard Harter. *Melville's Shorter Tales.* Norman: University of Oklahoma Press, 1960.

Franklin, H. Bruce. *The Wake of the Gods: Melville's Mythology.* Stanford: Stanford University Press, 1963.

Freeman, John. *Herman Melville.* London: Macmillan, 1926.

Geist, Stanley. *Herman Melville: The Tragic Vision and the Heroic Ideal.* Cambridge: Harvard University Press, 1939.

Gleim, W.S. *The Meaning of "Moby-Dick."* New York: Brick Row Bookshop, 1938. Reprint. New York: Russell & Russell, 1962.

Gross, Seymour L., ed. *A Benito Cereno Handbook.* Belmont, Calif: Wadsworth Publishing Co., 1965.

Guetti, James. *The Limits of Metaphor: A Study of Melville, Conrad and Faulkner.* Ithaca, N.Y.: Cornell University Press, 1967.

Hetherington. Hugh W. *Melville's Reviewers, British and American, 1846-1891.* Chapel Hill: University of North Carolina Press, 1961.

Hicks, Granville. "A Re-reading of *Moby-Dick,"* in *Twelve Original Essays on Great American Novels,* ed. Charles Shapiro. Detroit: Wayne State University Press, 1958, 44-68.

Hillway, Tyrus. *Herman Melville.* New York: Twayne Publishers, 1963.

Howard, Leon. *Herman Melville.* Minneapolis: University of Minnesota Press, 1961.

————. "Herman Melville, *Moby-Dick,"* in *The American Novel: From James Fenimore Cooper to William Faulkner,* ed. Wallace Stegner, New York: Basic Books, 1965, 25-34.

Humphreys, A.R. *Herman Melville.* New York: Grove Press, 1962.

James, C.L.R. *Mariners, Renegades, and Castaways: The Story of Herman Melville and the World We Live In.* New York: University Place Book Shop, 1953.

Levin, Harry. *The Power of Blackness: Hawthorne, Poe, Melville.* New York: Alfred A. Knopf, 1958.

Mansfield, Luther Stearns. "Some Patterns from Melville's 'Loom of Time,'" in *Essays on Determinism in American Literature,* ed. Sydney J. Krause. Kent, Ohio: Kent State University Press, 1964, 19-35.

Mason, Ronald. *The Spirit Above the Dust: A Study of Herman Melville.* London: John Lehmann, 1951.

Mayoux, Jean Jacques. *Melville.* trans. John Ashberry. New York: Grove Press, 1960.

Miller, James E. *A Reader's Guide to Herman Melville.* New York: Farrar, Straus & Giroux, 1962.

Miller, Perry. *The Raven and the Whale.* New York: Harcourt, Brace, 1956.

Munson, Gorham. *Style and Form in American Prose.* Port Washington, N.Y.: Kennikat Press, 1969.

Myers, Henry Alonzo. "The Tragic Meaning of *Moby-Dick,*" in *Tragedy: A View of Life.* Ithaca, N.Y.: Cornell University Press, 1956, 57-77.

O'Connor, William Van. "Plotinus Plinimmon and the Principle of Name-Giving," in *The Grotesque: An American Genre and Other Essays.* Carbondale: Southern Illinois University Press, 1962, 92-97.

Olson, Charles. *Call Me Ishmael.* New York: Reynal and Hitchcock, 1947. Reprint. New York: Grove Press, 1958.

Parker, Hershel, ed. *The Recognition of Herman Melville: Selected Criticism Since 1846.* Ann Arbor: University of Michigan Press, 1967.

Percival, M.O. *A Reading of "Moby-Dick."* Chicago: University of Chicago Press, 1950.

Pommer, Henry F. *Milton and Melville.* Pittsburgh: University of Pittsburgh Press, 1950.

Rosenberry, Edward Hoffman. *Melville and the Comic Spirit.* Cambridge: Harvard University Press, 1955.

Runden, John P., ed. *Melville's "Benito Cereno": A Text for Guided Research.* Boston: D.C. Heath, 1965.

Sealts, Merton M., Jr. *Melville's Reading: A Check-List of Books Owned and Borrowed.* Madison: University of Wisconsin Press, 1966.

Sedgwick, William Ellery. *Herman Melville: The Tragedy of Mind.* Cambridge: Harvard University Press, 1944.

Sewell, Richard B. *The Vision of Tragedy.* New Haven: Yale University Press, 1959.

Stafford, William T., ed. *Melville's "Billy Budd" and the Critics.* San Francisco: Wadsworth Publishing Co., 1961.

Stanonik, Janez. *Moby-Dick: The Myth and the Symbol. A Study in Folklore and Literature.* Ljubljana, Yugoslavia: Ljubljana University Press, 1962.

Stern, Milton R., ed. *Discussions of "Moby-Dick."* Boston: D.C. Heath, 1960.

——. *The Fine Hammered Steel of Herman Melville.* Urbana: University of Illinois Press, 1957.

Stewart, Randall, "Herman Melville, 1818-1891: Loyalty to the Heart," in

American Classics Reconsidered: A Christian Appraisal, ed. Harold C. Gardiner. New York: Charles Scribner's Sons, 1958, 210-228.

———. "The Vision of Evil in Hawthorne and Melville," in *The Tragic Vision and the Christian Faith,* ed. Nathan A. Scott, Jr. New York: Association Press, 1957, 238-263.

Stone, Geoffrey. *Melville.* New York: Sheed & Ward, 1949.

Thompson, Lawrance. *Melville's Quarrel with God.* Princeton: Princeton University Press, 1952.

Vincent, Howard P. *The Trying-Out of "Moby-Dick."* Boston: Houghton Mifflin, 1949. Reprint. Carbondale: Southern Illinois University Press, 1965.

———. *The Merrill Guide to Herman Melville.* Columbus, Ohio: Charles E. Merrill Books, 1969.

Wagner, Vern. "Billy Budd as Moby-Dick: An Alternate Reading," in *Studies in Honor of John Wilcox,* eds. A. Dayle Wallace and Woodburn O. Ross. Detroit: Wayne State University Press, 1958, 157-174.

Watkins, Floyd C. ."Melville's Plotinus Plinimmon and Pierre," in *Reality and Myth: Essays in American Literature in Memory of Richard Croom Beatty,* eds. William E. Walker and Robert L. Welker. Nashville: Vanderbilt University Press, 1964, 39-51.

Winters, Yvor. "Herman Melville and the Problems of Moral Navigation," in *Maule's Curse: Seven Studies in the History of American Obscurantism.* New York: New Directions, 1938, 53-89.

Wright, Nathalia. *Melville's Use of the Bible.* Durham, N.C.: Duke University Press, 1949.

Articles

General

Arvin, Newton. "Melville and the Gothic Novel," *Notes and Queries,* XXII (March 1949), 33-48.

Babcock, C. Merton. "The Language of Melville's 'Isolatoes,'" *Western Folklore,* X (October 1951), 285-289.

———. "Melville's World's Language," *Southern Folklore Quarterly,* XVI (September 1952), 177-182.

Bewley, Marius. "A Truce of God for Melville," *Sewanee Review,* LXI (Autumn 1953), 682-700.

Bezanson, Walter E. "Melville's Reading of Arnold's Poetry," *PMLA,* LXIX (June 1954), 365-391.

Braswell, William. "Melville as a Critic of Emerson," *American Literature,* IX (November 1937), 317-334.

Bridgman, Richard. "Melville's Roses," *Texas Studies in Literature and Language,* VIII (Summer 1966), 235-244.

Cannon, Agnes Dicken. "Melville's Use of Sea Ballads and Songs," *Western Folklore*, XXIII (January 1964), 1-16.

Carpenter, Frederic I. "Puritans Preferred Blondes: The Heroines of Melville and Hawthorne," *New England Quarterly*, IX (June 1936), 253-272.

Cecchi, Emilio. "Two Notes on Melville," *Sewanee Review*, LXVIII (July-September 1960), 398-406.

Charvat, William. "Melville and the Common Reader," *Studies in Bibliography*, XII (1959), 41-57.

Chase, Richard. "An Approach to Melville," *Partisan Review*, XIV (May-June 1947), 285-294.

Chittick, V.L.O. "The Way Back to Melville: Sea Chart of a Literary Revival," *Southwest Review*, XL (Summer 1955). 238-248.

Cohen, Hennig. "Wordplay on Personal Names in the Writings of Herman Melville," *Tennessee Studies in Literature*, VIII (1963), 85-97.

Davis, Merrell R. "Melville's Midwestern Lecture Tour," *Philological Quarterly*, XX (1959), 46-57.

Dix, William S. "Herman Melville and the Problem of Evil," *Revue Internationale de Philosophie*, XXV (July 1948), 81-107.

Donow, Herbert S. "Herman Melville and the Craft of Fiction," *Modern Language Quarterly*, XXV (June 1964), 181-186.

Duffy, Charles. "Toward the Whole Evidence on Melville as a Lecturer," *American Notes and Queries*, II (1942), 58.

Fadiman, Clifton, "Herman Melville," *Atlantic*, CLXXII (October 1943), 88-91.

Fagin, N.B. "Herman Melville and the Interior Monologue," *American Literature*, VII (January 1935), 433-434.

Fiess, Edward. "Melville as a Reader and Student of Byron," *American Literature*, XXIV (May 1952), 186-194.

Fiske, John C. "Herman Melville in Soviet Criticism," *Comparative Literature*, V (1953), 30-39.

Flanagan, John T. *"The Spirit of the Times* Reviews Melville," *Journal of English and Germanic Philology*, LXIV (January 1965), 57-64.

Forsythe, R.S. "Herman Melville in Honolulu," *New England Quarterly*, VIII (1935), 99-101.

Friedman, Maurice. "The Modern Job: On Melville, Dostoevsky, and Kafka," *Judaism*, XII (Fall 1963), 436-455.

Giono, Jean. "Pour saluer Melville," *Nouvelle Revue Francaise*, XXVIII, (1940), 433-468.

Glicksberg, Charles I. "Melville and the Negro Problem," *Phylon*, XI (III Quarter 1950), 207-215.

Gross, John J. "Melville, Dostoevsky and the People," *Pacific Spectator*, X

(Spring 1956), 160-170.

Hart, James D. "Melville and Dana," *American Literature,* IX (March 1937), 49-55.

Hayford, Harrison. "Hawthorne, Melville, and the Sea," *New England Quarterly,* XIX (December 1946), 435-452.

——. "The Significance of Melville's 'Agatha' Letters," *Journal of English Literary History,* XIII (December 1946), 299-310.

——. "Two New Letters of Herman Melville," *Journal of English Literary History,* XI (1944), 76-83.

——, and Merrell Davis. "Herman Melville as Office-Seeker," *Modern Language Quarterly,* X (June and September 1949), 168-183, 377-388.

Hayman, Allen. "The Real and the Original: Herman Melville's Theory of Prose Fiction," *Modern Fiction Studies,* VIII (Autumn 1962), 211-232.

Hillway, Tyrus. "A Note on Melville's Lecture in New Haven," *Modern Language Notes,* LX (1945), 55-57.

——. "Melville's Art: One Aspect," *Modern Language Notes,* LXII (November 1947), 477-480.

——. "Melville and the Spirit of Science," *South Atlantic Quarterly,* XLVIII (January 1949), 77-88.

——. "Melville's Geological Knowledge," *American Literature,* XXI (May 1949), 232-237.

——. "Melville's Use of Two Pseudo-Sciences," *Modern Language Notes,* LXIV (March 1950), 145-150.

——. "Melville as Critic of Science," *Modern Language Notes,* LXV (June 1950), 411-414.

——. "Melville as Amateur Zoologist," *Modern Language Quarterly,* XII (June 1951), 159-164.

Homans, George C. "The Dark Angel: The Tragedy of Herman Melville," *New England Quarterly,* V (October 1932), 699-730.

Howard, Leon. "Melville's Struggle with the Angel," *Modern Language Quarterly,* I (June 1940), 195-206.

Hughes, R.G. "Melville and Shakespeare," *Shakespeare Association Bulletin,* VII (July 1932), 103-112.

Hyman, Stanley Edgar. "Melville the Scrivener," *New Mexico Quarterly,* XXIII (Winter 1953), 381-415. Reprinted in *The Promised End: Essays and Reviews, 1942-1962.* New York: World, 1963.

Jerman, Bernard R. "With Real Admiration: More Correspondence between Melville and Bentley," *American Literature,* XXV (November 1953), 307-313.

Kazin, Alfred. "Ishmael and Ahab," *Atlantic,* CXCVIII (November 1956), 81-85.

Kligerman, Charles. "The Psychology of Herman Melville," *Psychoanalytic*

Review, XL (April 1953), 125-143.

Lacy, Patricia. "The Agatha Theme in Melville's Stories," *University of Texas Studies in English,* XXXV (1956), 96-105.

Leyda, Jay. "An Albany Journal of Gansevoort Melville," *Boston Public Library Quarterly,* II (October 1950), 327-347.

Lucas, F.L. "Herman Melville," *Die Neueren Sprachen,* XVIII (April 1922), 730-731.

Lucid, Robert F. "The Influence of *Two Years Before the Mast* on Herman Melville," *American Literature,* XXXI (November 1959), 243-256.

Lundkvist, Artur. "Herman Melville," *Bonniers Litterara Magasin,* XI (December 1942), 773-786.

MacDonald, Allan. "A Sailor among the Transcendentalists," *New England Quarterly,* VIII (September 1935), 307-319.

Mansfield, Luther Stearns. "Glimpses of Herman Melville's Life in Pittsfield, 1850-1851: Some Unpublished Letters of Evert A. Duyckinck," *American Literature,* IX (March 1937), 26-48.

――. "Melville's Comic Articles on Zachary Taylor," *American Literature,* IX (January 1938), 411-418.

Matteucci, G. "Herman Melville o delle ambiguita," *Vita e Pensiero,* XXV (February 1952), 401-408.

Miller, James. "Melville and Transcendentalism," *Virginia Quarterly Review,* XXIX (Autumn 1953), 556-575.

Miller, James E., Jr. "Hawthorne and Melville: The Unpardonable Sin," *PMLA,* LXX (March 1955), 91-111.

Morison, S.E. "Melville's Agatha Letter to Hawthorne," *New England Quarterly,* II (1929), 296-307.

Murray, Henry A. "In Nomine Diaboli," *New England Quarterly,* XXV (December 1951), 435-452.

Nichol, John W. "Melville and the Midwest," *PMLA,* LXVI (September 1951), 613-625.

Oates, J.C. "Melville and the Manichean Illusion," *Texas Studies in Literature and Language,* IV (Spring 1962), 117-129.

――. "Our Authors and Authorship: Melville and Curtis," *Putnam's Monthly,* IX (April 1957), 384-393.

Osborne, Frances Thomas. "Herman Melville Through a Child's Eyes," *Bulletin of the New York Public Library,* LXIX (December 1965), 655-660.

Parkes, Henry Bamford. "Poe, Hawthorne, Melville: An Essay in Sociological Criticism," *Partisan Review,* XVI (February 1949), 157-165.

Pattee, F.L. "Herman Melville," *American Mercury,* X (January 1927), 33-43.

Pommer, Henry F. "Herman Melville and the Wake of the *Essex,*" *Ameri-*

can Literature, XX (November 1948), 290-304.

Purcell, James M. "Melville's Contribution to English," *PMLA*, LVI (September 1941), 797-808.

Rahv, Philip. "Melville and His Critics," *Partisan Review*, XVII (Fall 1950), 732-775.

Rose, E.J. "Melville, Emerson, and the Sphinx," *New England Quarterly*, XXXVI (June 1963), 249-258.

Rosenheim, Frederick. "Flight from Home," *American Imago*, I (December 1940), 1-30.

Roudiez, Leon S. "Strangers in Melville and Camus," *French Review*, XXXI (January 1958), 217-226.

Sale, Arthur. "The Glass Ship: A Recurrent Image in Melville," *Modern Language Quarterly*, XVII (June 1956), 118-127.

Sealts, Merton M., Jr. "Did Melville Write 'October Mountain'?" *American Literature*, XXII (May 1950), 178-182.

———. "The Ghost of Major Melville," *New England Quarterly*, XXX (September 1957), 291-306.

———. "Melville's Burgundy Club Sketches," *Harvard Library Bulletin*, XII (Spring 1958), 253-267.

———. "Melville and the Shakers," *Studies in Bibliography*, II (1949-1950), 105-114.

———. "Melville's Neoplatonical Originals," *Modern Language Notes*, LXVII (1952), 80-86.

———. "The Publication of Melville's *Piazza Tales*," *Modern Language Notes*, LIX (January 1944), 56-59.

Slater, Judith. "The Domestic Adventurer in Melville's Tales," *American Literature*, XXXVII (November 1965), 267-279.

Star, Morris. "A Checklist of Portraits of Herman Melville," *Bulletin of the New York Public Library*, LXXI (September 1967), 468-473.

Stevens, Harry P. "Melville's Music," *Musicology*, II (July 1949), 405-421.

Thomas, Henre. "Herman Melville d'apres son Journal de Bord," *Critique*, VIII (October 1952), 833-846.

Van Doren, Carl. "Melville before the Mast," *Century Magazine*, CVIII (June 1924), 272-277.

Watters, Reginald E. "Melville's Metaphysics of Evil," *University of Toronto Quarterly*, IX (January 1940), 170-182.

———. "Melville's 'Sociality,'" *American Literature*, XVII (March 1945), 33-49.

———. "Melville's 'Isolatoes,'" *PMLA*, LX (December 1945), 1138-1148.

Weber, Walter. "Some Characteristic Symbols in Herman Melville's Works," *English Studies*, XXX (October 1949), 217-224.

Wright, Nathalia, "Biblical Allusions in Melville's Prose," *American Litera-*

ture, XII (1940), 185-199.

――――. "Form as Function in Melville," *PMLA*, LXVII (June 1952), 330-340.

Moby-Dick

Auden, W.H. "The Christian Tragic Hero," *New York Times Book Review*, December 16, 1945, p. 1.

Battenfield, David H. "The Source for the Hymn in *Moby-Dick*," *American Literature*, XXVII (November 1955), 393-396.

Beach, Joseph Warren. "Hart Crane and Moby-Dick," *Western Review*, XX (Spring 1956), 183-196.

Belgion, Montgomery. "Heterodoxy on *Moby-Dick*," *Sewanee Review*, LV (Winter 1947), 108-125.

Bell, Millicent, "Pierre Bayle and *Moby-Dick?*" *PMLA*, LXVI (September 1951), 626-648.

Booth, Thornton Y. *"Moby-Dick:* Standing Up to God," *Nineteenth-Century Fiction*, XVII (June 1962), 33-43.

Burgert, Hans. "William Faulkner on *Moby-Dick:* An Early Letter," *Studi Americani*, IX (1964), 371-375.

Cambon, Glauco. "Ishmael and the Problem of Formal Discontinuities in *Moby-Dick*," *Modern Language Notes*, LXXVI (June 1961), 516-523.

Canfield, Francis X. "Moby-Dick and the Book of Job," *Catholic World*, CLXXIV (January 1952), 254-260.

Colcord, Lincoln. "Notes on *Moby-Dick*," *Freeman*, V (August 23 and 30, 1922), 559-562, 585-587.

Cowan, S.A. "In Praise of Self-Reliance: The Role of Bulkington in *Moby-Dick*," *American Literature*, XXXVIII (January 1967), 547-556.

Dahl, C. *"Moby-Dick* and the Reviews of *The Cruise of the Cachelot*," *Modern Language Notes*, LXVII (November 1952), 471-471.

Dale, T.R. "Melville and Aristotle: The Conclusion of *Moby-Dick* as a Classical Tragedy," *Boston University Studies in English*, III (Spring 1957), 45-50.

Damon, S. Foster. "Why Ishmael Went to Sea," *American Literature*, II (1930), 281-283.

Duffy, Charles. "A Source for the Conclusion of Melville's *Moby-Dick*," *Notes and Queries*, CJXXXI (1941), 278-279.

[Eckardt.] Sister Mary Ellen. "Duplicate Imagery in *Moby-Dick*," *Modern Fiction Studies*, VIII (Autumn 1962), 252-264.

――――. "Parallels in Contrast: A Study of Melville's Imagery in *Moby-Dick* and *Billy Budd*," *Studies in Short Fiction*, II (Spring 1965), 284-290.

Farnsworth, Robert M. "Ishmael to the Royal Masthead," *University of Kansas City Review*, XXVIII (Spring 1962), 183-190.

Fast, Howard. "American Literature and the Democratic Tradition," *College English,* VIII (March 1947), 279-284.

Foster, Elizabeth S. "Another Note on Melville and Cetology," *American Literature,* XXII (January 1951), 479-487.

Friedrich, Gerhard. "A Note on Quakerism and *Moby-Dick:* Hawthorne's 'The Gentle Boy' as a Possible Source," *Quaker History,* LIV (Autumn 1965), 94-102.

Garnett, R.S. "Mocha-Dick, or the White Whale of the Pacific," *Times Literary Supplement,* July 30, 1926, p. 509.

——. "Moby-Dick and Mocha-Dick," *Blackwoods Magazine,* CCXXVI (December 1929), 841-858.

Geiger, Don. "Demonism in *Moby-Dick,*" *Perspective,* VI (Spring 1953), 111-124.

Gleim, W. S. "A Theory of *Moby-Dick,*" *New England Quarterly,* II (July 1929), 402-419.

Goldfard, Russell and Clare. "The Doubloon in *Moby-Dick,*" *Midwest Quarterly,* II (April 1961), 251-258.

Granger, Bruce Ingham. "The Gams in *Moby-Dick,*" *Western Humanities Review,* VIII (Winter 1953-1954), 41-47.

Grdseloff, Dorothee. "A Note on the Origin of Fedallah in *Moby-Dick,*" *American Literature,* XXVII (November 1955), 396-403.

Hall, James B. "*Moby-Dick*: Parable of a Dying System," *Western Review,* XIV (Spring 1950), 223-226.

Halverson, John. "The Shadow in *Moby-Dick,*" *American Quarterly,* XV (Fall 1963), 436-446.

Harding, Walter. "A Note on the Title 'Moby-Dick,'" *American Literature,* XXII (January 1951), 500-501.

Hefferman, William A. "Melville's Primitives: Queequeg and Fedallah," *Lock Haven Review,* Series 2, No. 1 (November 1964), 45-52.

Heflin, Wilson L. "The Source of Ahab's Lordship over the Level Loadstone," *American Literature,* XX (November 1948), 323-327.

Heimert, Alan. "*Moby-Dick* and American Political Symbolism," *American Quarterly,* XV (Winter 1963), 498-534.

Hoffman, Daniel G. "*Moby-Dick*: Jonah's Whale or Job's?" *Sewanee Review,* LXIX (Spring 1961), 205-224.

Hollis, Sophie. "*Moby-Dick:* A Religious Interpretation," *Catholic World,* CLXIII (May 1946), 158-162.

Holman, C. Hugh. "The Reconciliation of Ishmael: *Moby-Dick* and the Book of Job," *South Atlantic Quarterly,* LVII (Autumn 1958), 477-490.

Horsford, Howard D. "The Design of the Argument in *Moby-Dick,*" *Modern Fiction Studies,* VIII (Autumn 1962), 233-251.

Hull, William. *"Moby-Dick:* An Interpretation," *Etc.,* V (Autumn 1947), 8-21.

Hutchinson, William E. "A Definitive Edition of *Moby-Dick," American Literature,* XXV (January 1954), 472-478.

Jaffe, David. "Some Origins of *Moby-Dick:* New Finds in an Old Source," *American Literature,* XXIX (November 1957), 263-277.

———. "The Captain Who Sat for the Portrait of Ahab," *Boston University Studies in English,* IV (Spring 1960), 1-22.

Jones, Joseph. "'Ahab's Blood-Quench': Theater or Metallurgy?" *American Literature,* XVIII (March 1946), 35-37.

———. "Humor in *Moby-Dick," University of Texas Studies in English,* XXV (1945-1946), 51-71.

Kaplan, Sidney. "The *Moby-Dick* in the Service of the Underground Railroad," *Phylon,* XII (II Quarter 1951), 173-176.

———. "Herman Melville and the Whaling Enderbys," *American Literature,* XXIV (May 1952), 224-229.

Kirsch, James. "The Enigma of *Moby-Dick," Journal of Analytic Psychology,* III (Summer 1958), 131-148.

Koerner, James D. "The Wake of the White Whale," *Kansas Magazine,* (1954), 42-50.

Lash, Kenneth. "Captain Ahab and King Lear," *New Mexico Quarterly,* XIX (Winter 1949), 438-455.

Leiter, Louis. "Queequeg's Coffin," *Nineteenth-Century Fiction,* XIII (December 1958), 249-254.

Levin, Harry. "Don Quijote y Moby-Dick," *Realidad,* II (1947), 254-267.

Leyda, Jay. "Ishmael Melville: Remarks on Board of Ship *Amazon," Boston Public Library Quarterly,* I (October 1949), 119-134.

MacMechan, Archibald. "The Best Sea-Story Ever Written," *Queen's Quarterly,* VII (October 1899), 181-197.

McCloskey, J.C. *"Moby-Dick* and the Reviewers," *Philological Quarterly,* XXV (January 1946), 20-31.

Miller, Paul W. "Sun and Fire in Melville's *Moby-Dick," Nineteenth-Century Fiction,* XIII (September 1958), 139-144.

Millhauser, M. "The Form of *Moby-Dick," Journal of Aesthetics and Art Criticism,* XIII (June 1955), 527-532.

Mills, Gordon H. "The Castaway in *Moby-Dick," University of Texas Studies in English,* XXIX (1950), 231-248.

Mumford, L. "The Writing of *Moby-Dick," American Mercury,* XV (December 1928), 482-490.

Myers, Henry Alonzo. "Captain Ahab's Discovery: The Tragic Meaning of *Moby-Dick," New England Quarterly,* XV (1942), 15-34.

Osbourn, R.V. "The White Whale and the Absolute," *Essays in Criticism,*

VI (April 1956), 160-170.

Quinn, Patrick, F. "Poe's Imaginary Voyage," *Hudson Review,* IV (Winter 1952), 562-585.

Parke, John. "Seven *Moby-Dicks,*" *New England Quarterly,* XXVII (September 1955), 319-338.

Rockwell, Frederick S. "DeQuincey and the Ending of *Moby-Dick,*" *Nineteenth-Century Fiction,* IX (December 1954), 161-168.

Rosenfeld, William. "Uncertain Faith: Queequeg's Coffin and Melville's Use of the Bible," *Texas Studies in Literature and Language,* VII (Winter 1966), 317-327.

Schless, Howard H. "Moby-Dick and Dante: A Critique and Time Scheme," *Bulletin of the New York Public Library,* LXV (May 1961), 289-312.

Scott, Sumner, W.D. "Some Implications of the Typhoon Scenes in *Moby-Dick,*" *American Literature,* XII (March 1940), 91-98.

Seelye, John D. "The Golden Navel: The Cabalism of Ahab's Doubloon," *Nineteenth-Century Fiction,* XIV (March 1960), 350-355.

Shulman, Robert. "Melville's Thomas Fuller: An Outline for Starbuck and an Instance of the Creator as Critic," *Modern Language Quarterly,* XXIII (December 1962), 337-352.

——. "The Serious Function of Melville's Phallic Jokes," *American Literature,* XXXIII (May 1961), 179-194.

Slochower, Harry. "Freudian Motifs in *Moby-Dick,*" *Complex* #3, (Fall 1950), 16-25.

Stavrou, C.N. "Ahab and Dick Again," *Texas Studies in Literature and Language,* III (Autumn 1961), 309-320.

Stern, Milton R. "The Whale and the Minnow," *College English,* XVII (May 1956), 470-473.

Stoll, Elmer E. "Symbolism in *Moby-Dick,*" *Journal of the History of Ideas,* XII (June 1951), 440-465.

Tucker, Harry, Jr. "A Glance at 'Whiteness' in Melville and Camus," *PMLA,* LXXX (December 1965), 605.

Van Doren, Carl. "Mr. Melville's Moby-Dick," *Bookman* (American), LIX (April 1924), 154-157.

Vargish, Thomas. "Gnostick *Mythos* in *Moby-Dick,*" *PMLA,* LXXXI (June 1966), 272-277.

Watson, E.L. Grant. "Moby-Dick," *London Mercury,* III (December 1920), 180-186.

Watters, R.E. "The Meanings of the White Whale," *University of Toronto Quarterly,* XX (January 1951), 155-161.

Watts, Robert A. "The 'Seaward Peep': Ahab's Transgression," *University Review,* XXXI (December 1964), 133-138.

Weathers, Willie T. *"Moby-Dick* and the Nineteenth-Century Scene," *Texas Studies in Literature and Language,* I (Winter 1960), 477-501.

Woodson, Thomas. "Ahab's Greatness: Prometheus as Narcissus," *Journal of English Literary History,* XXXIII (September 1966), 351-369.

Wright, Nathalia. "Moby-Dick: Jonah's or Job's Whale?" *American Literature,* XXXVII (May 1965), 190-195.

———. *"Mosses from an Old Manse* and *Moby-Dick:* The Shock of Discovery," *Modern Language Notes,* LXVII (June 1952), 387-392.

Young, James Dean. "The Nine Gams of the Pequod," *American Literature,* XXV (January 1954), 449-463.

Yu, Beongcheon. "Ishmael's Equal Eye: The Source of Balance in *Moby-Dick,"* *Journal of English Literary History,* XXXII (March 1965), 110-125.

Billy Budd

Anderson, Charles R. "The Genesis of *Billy Budd,"* *American Literature,* XII (November 1940), 329-346.

Anderson, Quentin. "Second Trip to Byzantium," *Kenyon Review,* XI (Summer 1949), 516-520.

Barnet, Sylvan. "The Execution in *Billy Budd,"* *American Literature,* XXXIII (January 1962), 517-519.

Brodtkorb, Paul, Jr. "The Definitive *Billy Budd:* 'But Aren't It All Sham?'" *PMLA,* LXXXII (December 1967), 602-612.

Browne, Ray B. *"Billy Budd:* Gospel of Democracy," *Nineteenth-Century Fiction,* XVII (March 1963), 321-337.

Campbell, Harry Modean. "The Hanging Scene in Melville's *Billy Budd Foretopman,"* *Modern Language Notes,* LXVI (June 1951), 378-381.

Casper, Leonard. "The Case Against Captain Vere," *Perspective,* V (Summer 1952), 146-152.

Chandler, Alice. "Captain Vere and the 'Tragedies of the Palace,'" *Modern Fiction Studies,* XIII (Summer 1967), 259-261.

Cramer, Maurice B. *"Billy Budd* and *Billy Budd,"* *Journal of General Education,* X (April 1957), 78-91.

Duerksen, Roland A. *Caleb Williams, Political Justice,* and *Billy Budd,"* *American Literature,* XXXVIII (November 1966), 372-376.

Fogle, Richard H. *"Billy Budd:* The Order of the Fall," *Nineteenth-Century Fiction,* XV (December 1960), 189-205.

Freimarck, Vincent. "Mainmast as Crucifix in *Billy Budd,"* *Modern Language Notes,* LXXII (November·1957), 496-497.

Goldsmith, Arnold L. "The 'Discovery Scene' in *Billy Budd,"* *Modern Drama,* III (February 1961), 339-342.

Gollin, Richard Andrita. "Justice in an Earlier Treatment of the *Billy Budd* Theme," *American Literature,* XXVIII (January 1957), 513-515.

Hall, Joan Joffe. "The Historical Chapters in *Billy Budd,*" *University Review,* XXX (October 1963), 35-40.

Hillway, Tyrus. "*Billy Budd:* Melville's Human Sacrifice," *Pacific Spectator,* VI (Summer 1952), 342-347. .

Hudson, H.E. "Billy Budd: Adam or Christ?" *The Crane Review,* VII (Winter 1965), 62-67.

Kilbourne, W.G., Jr. "Montaigne and Captain Vere," *American Literature,* XXXIII (January 1962), 514-517.

Ledbetter, Kenneth. "The Ambiguity of *Billy Budd,*" *Texas Studies in Literature and Language,* IV (Spring 1962), 130-134.

Lemon, Lee T. "*Billy Budd:* The Plot Against the Story," *Studies in Short Fiction,* II (Fall 1964), 32-43.

London, Philip W. "The Military Necessity: *Billy Budd* and Vigny," *Comparative Literature,* XIV (Spring 1962), 174-186.

McCarthy, Paul. Character and Structure in *Billy Budd,*" *Discourse,* IX (Spring 1966), 201-217.

McElderry, B.R., Jr. "Three Earlier Treatments of the *Billy Budd* Theme," *American Literature,* XXVII (May 1955), 251-257.

Montale, Eugenio. "An Introduction to *Billy Budd* (1942)," *Sewanee Review,* LXVIII (July-September 1960), 419-422.

Phelps, Leland R. "The Reaction to *Benito Cereno* and *Billy Budd* in Germany," *Symposium,* XIII (Fall 1959), 294-299.

Rathbun, John W. *Billy Budd* and the Limits of Perception," *Nineteenth-Century Fiction,* XX (June 1965), 19-34.

Reist, John S., Jr. "Surd Evil and Suffering Love," *Universitas,* II (1964), 81-90.

Rogers, Robert. "The 'Ineludible Gripe' of *Billy Budd,*" *Literature and Psychology,* XIV (Winter 1964), 9-22.

Rosenberry, Edward H. "The Problem of *Billy Budd,*" *PMLA,* LXXX (December 1965), 489-498.

Sale, Arthur. "Captain Vere's Reasons," *Cambridge Journal,* V (October 1951), 3-18.

Schiffman, Joseph. "Melville's Final Stage, Irony: A Re-examination of *Billy Budd* Criticism," *American Literature,* XXII (May 1950), 128-136.

Seelye, John D. "'Spontaneous Impress of Truth': Melville's Jack Chase: A Source, an Analogue, A Conjecture,'" *Nineteenth-Century Fiction,* XX (March 1966), 367-376.

Shattuck, Roger. "Two Inside Narratives: *Billy Budd* and *L'Etranger,*"

Texas Studies in Literature and Language, IV (Autumn 1962), 314-320.

Sherwood, John C. "Vere as Collingwood: A Key to *Billy Budd,*" *American Literature,* XXXV (January 1964), 476-484.

Shulman, Robert. "Melville's 'Timoleon': From Plutarch to the Early Stages of *Billy Budd,*" *Comparative Literature,* XIX (Fall 1967), 351-361.

——. "Montaigne and the Techniques and Tragedy of Melville's *Billy Budd,*" *Comparative Literature,* XVI (Fall 1964), 322-330.

Stein, William Bysshe. "*Billy Budd:* The Nightmare of History," *Criticism,* III (Summer 1961), 237-250.

——. "The Motif of the Wise Old Man in *Billy Budd,*" *Western Humanities Review,* XIV (Winter 1960), 99-101.

Sutton, Walter. "Melville and the Great God Budd," *Prairie Schooner,* XXXIV (Summer 1960), 128-133.

Weir, Charles, Jr. "Malice Reconciled: A Note on Herman Melville's *Billy Budd,*" *University of Toronto Quarterly,* XIII (April 1944), 276-285.

West, Ray B., Jr. "The Unity of *Billy Budd,*" *Hudson Review,* V (Spring 1952), 120-127.

White, Edgar Walter. "*Billy Budd,*" *Adelphi,* XXVIII (I Quarter 1952), 492-498.

Widmer, Kingsley. "The Perplexed Myths of Melville: *Billy Budd,*" *Novel,* II (Fall 1968), 23-35.

Wilson, G.R., Jr. "*Billy Budd* and Melville's Use of Dramatic Technique," *Studies in Short Fiction,* IV (Winter 1967), 105-111.

Withim, Phil. "*Billy Budd:* Testament of Resistance," *Modern Language Quarterly,* XX (June 1959), 115-127.

Zink, Karl E. "Herman Melville and the Forms, Irony and Social Criticisms in *Billy Budd,*" *Accent,* XII (Summer 1952), 131-139.

The Confidence-Man

Drew, Philip. "Appearance and Reality in Melville's *The Confidence-Man,*" *Journal of English Literary History,* XXXI (December 1964), 418-442.

Grauman, Lawrence, Jr. "Suggestions on the Future of *The Confidence-Man,*" *Papers on Language and Literature,* I (Summer 1965), 241-249.

Hayford, Harrison. "Poe in *The Confidence-Man,*" *Nineteenth-Century Fiction,* XIV (December 1959), 207-218.

Hoffman, Daniel G. "Melville's 'Story of China Aster,'" *American Literature,* XXII (May 1950), 137-149.

Horsford, Howard C. "Evidence of Melville's Plans for a Sequel to *The Confidence-Man,*" *American Literature.,* XXIV (1952), 85-88.

Karcner, Carolyn Lury. "The Story of Charlemont: A Dramatization of Melville's Concepts of Fiction in *The Confidence-Man: His Masquerade,*" *Nineteenth-Century Fiction,* XXI (June 1966), 73-84.

McCarthy, Paul. "The 'Soldier of Fortune' in Melville's *The Confidence-Man,*" *Emerson Society Quarterly,* No. 33 (IV Quarter 1963), 21-24.

Oliver, Egbert S. "Melville's Goneril and Fanny Kemble," *New England Quarterly,* XVIII (December 1945), 489-500.

———. "Melville's Picture of Emerson and Thoreau in *The Confidence-Man,*" *College English,* VIII (November 1946), 61-72.

Orth, Ralph H. "An Early Review of *The Confidence-Man,*" *Emerson Society Quarterly,* No. 43 (II Quarter 1966), 48.

Parker, Hershel. "The Metaphysics of Indian-Hating," *Nineteenth-Century Fiction,* XVIII (September 1963), 165-173.

Pearce, Roy Harvey. "Melville's Indian-Hater: A Note on the Meaning of *The Confidence-Man,*" *PMLA,* LXVII (December 1952), 942-948.

Reeves, Paschal. "The 'Deaf-Mute' Confidence-Man: Melville's Imposter in Action," *Modern Language Notes,* LXXV (January 1960), 18-20.

Seelye, John D. "Timothy Flint's 'Wicked River' and *The Confidence-Man,*" *PMLA,* LXXVIII (March 1963), 75-79.

Schroeder, John W. "Sources and Symbols for Melville's *Confidence-Man,*" *PMLA,* LXVI (June 1951), 363-380.

Smith, Paul. "*The Confidence-Man* and the Literary World of New York," *Nineteenth-Century Fiction,* XVI (March 1962), 329-337.

Tuveson, Ernest. "The Creed of the Confidence-Man," *Journal of English Literary History,* XXXIII (June 1966), 247-270.

Wright, Nathalia. "The Confidence-Men of Melville and Cooper: An American Indictment," *American Quarterly,* IV (Fall 1952), 266-268.

Pierre

Braswell, William. "The Satirical Temper of Melville's *Pierre,*" *American Literature,* VII (January 1936), 424-438.

———. "Melville's Opinion of *Pierre,*" *American Literature,* XXIII (May 1951), 246-250.

Bush, C.W. "This Stupendous Fabric: The Metaphysics of Order in Melville's *Pierre* and Nathanael West's *Miss Lonelyhearts,*" *Journal of American Study,* I (October 1967), 269-274.

Damon, S. Foster. *Pierre* and the Ambiguous," *Hound and Horn,* II (January-March 1929), 107-118.

Dauner, Louise. "The 'Case' of Tobias Pearson: Hawthorne and the Ambiguities," *American Literature,* XXI (January 1950), 464-472.

Dichmann, Mary E. "Absolutism in Melville's *Pierre,*" *PMLA,* LXVII (September 1952), 702-715.

Forsythe, Robert S. "Mr. Lewis Mumford and Melville's *Pierre,*" *American Literature,* II (November 1930), 286-289.

Giovannini, G. "Melville's *Pierre* and Dante's *Inferno,*" *PMLA,* LXIV (March 1949), 70-78.

Gupta, R.K. "Melville's Use of Non-Novelistic Conventions in *Pierre,*" *Emerson Society Quarterly,* No. 48 (III Quarter 1967), 141-145.

Kimmey, John L. "Pierre and Robin: Melville's Debt to Hawthorne," *Emerson Society Quarterly,* No. 38 (I Quarter 1965), 90-92.

Kissane, James. "Imagery, Myth, and Melville's *Pierre,*" *American Literature,* XXVI (January 1955), 564-572.

Logan, John. "Psychological Motifs in Melville's *Pierre,*" *Minnesota Review,* VII (1967), 325-330.

Lueders, Edward G. "The Melville-Hawthorne Relationship in *Pierre* and *The Blithedale Romance,*" *Western Humanities Review,* IV (Autumn 1950), 323-334.

McCorquodale, Marjorie Kimball. "Melville's Pierre as Hawthorne," *University of Texas Studies in English,* XXXIII (1954), 97-102.

Moorman, Charles. "Melville's Pierre in the City," *American Literature,* XXVII (January 1956), 571-577.

Schless, Howard H. "Flaxman, Dante, and Melville's *Pierre,*" *Bulletin of the New York Public Library,* LXIV (February 1960), 65-82.

Turner, Darwin T. "A View from Melville's 'Piazza,'" *College Language Association Journal,* VII (September 1963), 56-62.

Watson, E.L. Grant. "Melville's Pierre," *New England Quarterly,* III (April 1930), 195-234.

Yaggy, Elinor. "Shakespeare and Melville's *Pierre,*" *Boston Public Library Quarterly,* VI (January 1954), 43-51.

Mardi

Blansett, Barbara N. "'From Dark to Dark': *Mardi,* a Foreshadowing of *Pierre,*" *The Southern Quarterly,* I (April 1963), 213-227.

Braswell, William. "Melville's Use of Seneca," *American Literature,* XII (March 1940), 98-104.

Davis, Merrell R. "The Flower Symbolism in *Mardi,*" *Modern Language Quarterly,* II (1942), 625-638.

Hillway, Tyrus. "Taji's Abdication in Herman Melville's *Mardi,*" *American Literature,* XVI (1944), 204-207.

Jaffe, David. "Some Sources of Melville's *Mardi,*" *American Literature,* IX (March 1937), 56-69.

Larrabee, Stephen A. "Melville Against the World," *South Atlantic Quarterly,* XXXIV (October 1935), 410-418.

Levine, Stuart. "Melville's 'Voyage Thither,'" *Midwest Quarterly*, III (July 1962), 341-353.

Wright, Nathalia. "A Note on Melville's Use of Spenser: Hautia and the Bower of Bliss," *American Literature*, XXIV (March 1952), 83-85.

Redburn

Bercovitch, Sacvan. "Melville's Search for National Identity: Son and Father in *Redburn, Pierre*, and *Billy Budd,*" *College Language Association Journal*, X (March 1967), 217-228.

Bowen, Merlin. *"Redburn* and the Angle of Vision," *Modern Philology*, LII (November 1954), 100-109.

Franklin, H. Bruce. "Redburn's Wicked End," *Nineteenth-Century Fiction*, XX (September 1965), 190-194.

Huntress, Keith. "A Note on Melville's *Redburn,"* *New England Quarterly*, XVIII (1945), 259-260.

White-Jacket

Anderson, Charles R. "A Reply to Melville's *White-Jacket* by Rear-Admiral Thomas O. Selfridge, Sr.," *American Literature*, VII (May 1935), 123-144.

Heflin, Wilson L. "A Man-of-War Button Divides Two Cousins," *Boston Public Library Quarterly*, III (January 1951), 51-60.

McCarthy, Paul. "Symbolic Elements in *White-Jacket,"* *Midwest Quarterly*, VII (July 1966), 309-325.

Nichol, John W. "Melville's '"Soiled" Fish of the Sea,'" *American Literature*, XXI (November 1949), 338-339.

Philbrick, Thomas L. "Another Source for *White-Jacket*," *American Literature*, XXIX (January 1958), 431-439.

——. "Melville's 'Best Authorities,'" *Nineteenth-Century Fiction*, XV (September 1960), 171-179.

Zirker, Priscilla Allen. "Evidence of the Slavery Dilemma in *White-Jacket,"* *American Quarterly*, XVIII (Fall 1966), 477-492.

Typee

Anderson, Charles R. "Contemporary American Opinions of *Typee* and *Omoo,"* *American Literature*, IX (March 1937), 1-25.

——. "Melville's English Debut," *American Literature*, XI (March 1939), 23-38.

Beatty, Lillian. "Typee and Blithedale: Rejected Ideal Communities," *The Personalist*, XXXVII (Autumn 1956), 367-378.

DeVoto, Bernard. "Editions of *Typee,"* *Saturday Review of Literature*, November 24, 1928, p. 406.

Gohdes, Clarence. "Melville's Friend 'Toby,'" *Modern Language Notes,* LIX (January 1944), 52-55.

Haraszti, Zoltan. "Melville Defends Typee," *Bulletin of the Boston Public Library,* XX (June 1947), 203-208.

Houghton, Donald E. "The Incredible Ending of Melville's *Typee,*" *Emerson Society Quarterly,* No. 22 (I Quarter 1961), 28-31.

Petrullo, Helen B. "The Neurotic Hero of *Typee,*" *American Imago,* XII (1955), 317-323.

Scudder, Harold H. "Hawthorne's Use of *Typee,*" *Notes and Queries,* CLXXXVII (October 21, 1944), 184-186.

Stanton, Robert. "*Typee* and Milton: Paradise Well Lost," *Modern Language Notes,* LXXIV (May 1959), 407-411.

Tanselle, G. Thomas. "The First Review of *Typee,*" *American Literature,* XXXIV (January 1963), 567-571.

Williams, Mentor L. "Some Notices and Reviews of Melville's Novels in American Religious Periodicals, 1846-1849," *American Literature,* XXII (May 1950), 119-127.

Omoo

Anderson, Charles R. "Contemporary American Opinions of *Typee* and *Omoo,*" *American Literature,* IX (March 1937), 1-25.

———. "Melville's English Debut," *American Literature,* IX (March 1939), 23-28.

Kaplan, Sidney. "'Omoo,' Melville's and Boucicault's," *American Notes and Queries,* VIII (January 1950), 150-151.

Leeson, Ida. "Mutiny on the *Lucy Ann,*" *Philological Quarterly,* XIX (October 1940), 370-379.

Israel Potter

Frederick, John T. "Symbol and Theme in Melville's *Israel Potter,*" *Modern Fiction Studies,* VIII (Autumn 1962), 265-275.

Jackson, Kenny. "Israel Potter: Melville's 'Fourth of July Story,'" *College Language Association Journal,* VI (March 1963), 194-204.

Rosenberry, Edward H. "Israel Potter, Benjamin Franklin, and the Doctrine of Self-Reliance," *Emerson Society Quarterly,* No. 28 (III Quarter 1962), 27-29.

Russell, Jack. "*Israel Potter* and 'Song of Myself,'" *American Literature,* XL (March 1968), 72-77.

Yates, Norris. "An Instance of Parallel Imagery in Hawthorne, Melville, and Frost," *Philological Quarterly,* XXXVI (April 1957), 276-280.

"Benito Cereno"

Bernstein, John. "'Benito Cereno' and the Spanish Inquisition," *Nineteenth-Century Fiction*, XVI (March 1962), 345-350.

Cardwell, Guy. "Melville's Gray Story: Symbols and Meaning in 'Benito Cereno,'" *Bucknell Review*, VIII (May 1959), 154-167.

Carlisle, E.F. "Captain Amasa Delano: Melville's American Fool," *Criticism*, VII (Fall 1965), 349-362.

D'Azevedo, Warren. "Revolt on the *San Dominick,*" *Phylon*, XVII (II Quarter 1956), 129-140.

Feltenstein, Rosalie. "Melville's 'Benito Cereno,'" *American Literature*, XIX (November 1947), 245-255.

Fogle, Richard H. "The Monk and the Bachelor: Melville's 'Benito Cereno,'" *Tulane Studies in English*, III (1953), 155-178.

Franklin, H. Bruce. "'Apparent Symbol of Despotic Command': Melville's 'Benito Cereno,'" *New England Quarterly*, XXXIV (December 1961), 462-477.

Glicksberg, Charles I. "Melville and the Negro Problem," *Phylon*, XI (III Quarter 1950), 207-215.

Green, Jesse D. "Diabolism, Pessimism, and Democracy: Notes on Melville and Conrad," *Modern Fiction Studies*, VIII (Autumn 1962), 287-305.

Gross, Seymour L. "Mungo Park and Ledyard in Melville's 'Benito Cereno,'" *English Language Notes*, III (December 1965), 122-123.

Guttmann, Allen. "The Enduring Innocence of Captain Amasa Delano," *Boston University Studies in English*, V (Spring 1961), 35-45.

Haber, Tom Burns. "A Note on Melville's 'Benito Cereno,'" *Nineteenth-Century Fiction*, VI (September 1951), 146-147. See also Ward Pafford and Floyd C. Watkins, "'Benito Cereno': A Note in Rebuttal," *Nineteenth-Century Fiction*, VII (June 1952), 68-71.

Jackson, Margaret Y. "Melville's Use of a Real Slave Mutiny in 'Benito Cereno,'" *College Language Association Journal*, IV (December 1960), 79-93.

Kaplan, Sidney. "Herman Melville and the American National Sin: The Meaning of 'Benito Cereno,'" *Journal of Negro History*, XLI (October 1956), 311-338, and XLII (January 1957), 11-37.

Keeler, Clinton. "Melville's Delano: Our Cheerful Axiologist," *College Language Association Journal*, X (September 1966), 49-55.

Knox, George. "Lost Command: 'Benito Cereno' Reconsidered," *The Personalist*, LX (Summer 1959), 280-291.

Pafford, Ward, and Floyd C. Watkins. "'Benito Cereno': A Note in Rebuttal," *Nineteenth-Century Fiction*, VII (June 1952), 68-71.

Phillips, Barry. "'The Good Captain': A Reading of 'Benito Cereno,'". *Texas Studies in Literature and Language,* IV (Summer 1962), 188-197.

Pilkington, William T. "'Benito Cereno' and the American National Character," *Discourse,* VIII (Winter 1965), 49-63.

——. "'Benito Cereno' and the 'Valor-Ruined Man' of *Moby-Dick,*" *Texas Studies in Literature and Language,* VII (Summer 1965), 201-207.

——. "Melville's 'Benito Cereno': Source and Technique," *Studies in Short Fiction,* II (Spring 1965), 247-255.

Ridge, George Ross and Davy S. "A Bird and a Motto: Source for 'Benito Cereno,'" *Mississippi Quarterly,* XII (Winter 1959-1960), 22-29.

Rohrberger, Mary. "Point of View in 'Benito Cereno': Machinations and Deceptions," *College English,* XXVII (April 1965), 541-546.

Schiffman, Joseph. "Critical Problems in Melville's 'Benito Cereno,'" *Modern Language Quarterly,* XI (September 1950), 317-324.

Scudder, Harold H. "Melville's 'Benito Cereno' and Captain Delano's Voyages," *PMLA,* XLIII (June 1928), 502-532.

Stein, William Bysshe. "The Moral Axis of 'Benito Cereno,'" *Accent,* XV (Summer 1955), 221-233.

Turner, Darwin T. "A View of Melville's 'Piazza,'" *College Language Association Journal,* VII (September 1963), 61-62.

Widmer, Kingsley. "The Perplexity of Melville: 'Benito Cereno,'" *Studies in Short Fiction,* V (Spring 1968), 225-238.

Williams, Stanley T. "'Follow Your Leader': Melville's 'Benito Cereno,'" *Virginia Quarterly Review,* XXIII (Winter 1947), 61-76.

"Bartleby"

Eliot, Alexander. "Melville and Bartleby," *Furioso,* III (Fall 1947), 11-21.

Felheim, Marvin. "Meaning and Structure in 'Bartleby,'" *College English,* XXIII (February 1962), 369-370, 375-376.

Gardner, John. "Bartleby: Art and Social Commitment," *Philological Quarterly,* XLIII (January 1964), 87-98.

Marcus, Mordecai. "Melville's Bartleby as a Psychological Double," *College English,* XXIII (February 1962), 365-368.

Marx, Leo. "Melville's Parable of the Walls," *Sewanee Review,* LXI (Autumn 1953), 602-627.

Spector, Robert D. "Melville's 'Bartleby' and the Absurd," *Nineteenth-Century Fiction,* XVI (September 1961), 175-177.

Widmer, Kingsley. "The Negative Affirmation: Melville's 'Bartleby,'" *Modern Fiction Studies,* VIII (Autumn 1962), 276-286.

Miscellaneous

Chatfield, E. Hale. "Levels of Meaning in Melville's 'I and My Chimney,'" *American Imago,* XIX (Summer 1962), 163-169.

Crowley, William G. "Melville's Chimney," *Emerson Society Quarterly,* No. 14 (I Quarter 1959), 2-6.

Davidson, Frank. "Melville, Thoreau, and 'The Apple-Tree Table,'" *American Literature,* XXV (January 1954), 479-488.

Eby, E.H. "Herman Melville's 'Tartarus of Maids,'" *Modern Language Quarterly,* I (March 1940), 95-100.

Fisher, Marvin. "Melville's 'Bell-Tower': A Double Thrust," *American Quarterly,* XVIII (Summer 1966), 200-207.

——. "Melville's 'Jimmy Rose': Truly Risen?" *Studies in Short Fiction,* IV (Fall 1966), 1-11.

Franklin, H. Bruce. "The Island Worlds of Darwin and Melville," *The Centennial Review,* XI (Summer 1967), 353-370.

Gargano, James W. "Melville's 'Jimmy Rose,'" *Western Humanities Review,* XVI (Summer 1962), 276-280.

Howard, Leon. "Melville and Spenser—A Note on Criticism," *Modern Language Notes,* XLVI (May 1931), 291-292.

Jones, Buford. "Spenser and Shakespeare in 'The Encantadas,' Sketch VI," *Emerson Society Quarterly,* XXXV (II Quarter 1964), 68-73.

Kimpel, Ben D. "Melville's 'The Lightning-Rod Man,'" *American Literature,* XVI (March 1944), 30-32.

Magaw, Malcolm O. "Apocalyptic Imagery in Melville's 'The Apple-Tree Table,'" *Midwest Quarterly,* VIII (July 1967), 357-369.

Newberry, I. "'The Encantadas': Melville's *Inferno,*" *American Literature,* XXXVIII (March 1966), 49-68.

Oliver, Egbert S. "'Cock-A-Doodle-Doo!' and Transcendental Hocus-Pocus," *New England Quarterly,* XXI (June 1948), 204-216.

——. "Herman Melville's Lightning-Rod Man," *The Philadelphia Forum,* XXXV (June 1956), 4-5, 17.

——. "Melville's 'Tartarus,'" *Emerson Society Quarterly,* No. 28 (II Quarter 1962), 23-25.

Parker, Hershel. "Melville's Salesman Story," *Studies in Short Fiction,* I (Winter 1964), 154-158.

Pearce, Howard D. "The Narrator of 'Norfolk Isle and the Chola Widow,'" *Studies in Short Fiction,* III (Fall 1965), 56-62.

Resink, G.J. "Samburan Encantada," *English Studies,* XLVII (February 1966), 35-44.

Sackman, Douglas. "The Original of Melville's Apple-Tree Table," *American Literature,* XI (January 1940), 448-451.

Sowder, William J. "Melville's 'I and My Chimney: A Southern Exposure,'" *Mississippi Quarterly*, XVI (Summer 1963), 128-145.

Stein, William Bysshe. "Melville's Eros," *Texas Studies in Literature and Language*, III (Autumn 1961), 297-308.

——. "Melville's Chimney Chivy," *Emerson Society Quarterly*, No. 35 (II Quarter 1964), 63-65.

Stockton, Eric W. "A Commentary of Melville's 'The Lightning-Rod Man,'" *Papers of the Michigan Academy of Science, Arts, and Letters*, XL (1955), 321-328.

Thomas, Russell. "Melville's Use of Some Sources in 'The Encantadas,'" *American Literature*, III (January 1932), 432-456.

Thompson, W.R. "Melville's 'The Fiddler': A Study in Dissolution," *Texas Studies in Literature and Language*, II (Winter 1961), 492-500.

Turner, Darwin T. "Smoke from Melville's Chimney," *College Language Association Journal*, VII (December 1963), 107-113.

Tutt, Ralph M. "'Jimmy Rose'—Melville's Displaced Noble," *Emerson Society Quarterly*, No. 33 (IV Quarter 1963), 28-32.

Woodruff, Stuart C. "Melville and His Chimney," *PMLA*, LXXV (June 1960), 283-292.

Poetry

Arvin, Newton. "Melville's *Clarel*," *Hudson Review*, XIV (Summer·1961), 298-300.

Ault, Nelson A. "The Sea Imagery in Herman Melville's *Clarel*," *Research Studies of the State College of Washington*, XXVII (June 1959), 72-84.

Berlind, Bruce. "Notes on Melville's Shorter Poems," *Hopkins Review*, III (Summer 1950), 24-35.

Dillingham, William B. "'Neither Believer Nor Infidel': Themes of Melville's Poetry," *The Personalist*, XLVI (October 1965), 501-516.

Fogle, Richard H. "Melville and the Civil War," *Tulane Studies in English*, IX (1959), 61-89.

Hand, Harry E. "'And War Be Done': *Battle-Pieces* and Other Civil War Poetry of Herman Melville," *Journal of Human Relations*, XI (Spring 1963), 326-340.

Levy, Leo B. "Hawthorne, Melville, and the *Monitor*," *American Literature*, XXXVII (March 1965), 33-40.

Lindeman, Jack. "Herman Melville's Civil War," *Modern Age*, IX (Fall 1965), 387-398.

Mabbott, Thomas O. "Poem by Herman Melville," *Notes and Queries*, CXLIX (July 18, 1925), 42-43.

——. "Melville's 'A Railroad Cutting Near Alexandria in 1855,'" *Explicator*, IX (June 1951), item 55.

Shaw, Richard O. "The Civil War Poems of Herman Melville," *Lincoln Herald*, LXVIII (Spring 1966), 44-49.

Shulman, Robert. "Melville's *Timoleon:* From Plutarch to the Early Stages of *Billy Budd,*" *Comparative Literature*, XIX (Fall 1967), 351-361.

Stein, William Bysshe. "Melville's Poetry: Its Symbols of Individuation," *Literature and Psychology*, VII (May 1957), 21-26.

——. "The Old Man and the Triple Goddess: Melville's 'The Haglets,'" *Journal of English Literary History*, XXV (March 1958), 43-59.

Tilton, Eleanor M. "Melville's 'Rammon': A Text and Commentary," *Harvard Library Bulletin*, XIII (Winter 1959), 50-91.

Warren, Robert Penn. "Melville the Poet," *Kenyon Review*, VIII (Spring 1946), 208-223.

Wells, Henry W. "Herman Melville's *Clarel,*" *College English*, IV (May 1943), 478-483.

Wright, Nathalia. "A Source for Melville's *Clarel:* Dean Stanley's 'Sinai and Palestine,'" *Modern Language Notes*, LXII (February 1947), 110-116.

Index of Authors